SQL

The Most Up-To-Date Guide For Beginners To Learn SQL Programming

TABLE OF CONTENTS

INTRODUCTION

SQL stands for Structured Query Language and it is the lingua franca in the database community. SQL is a standard which is utilized by all database vendors and programmers to explain, extract and access the info that is kept in databases.

SQL started existence as an IBM development but was standardized by (ANSI) the American National Standards Institute and (ISO) the International Organization for Standardization as ANSI/ISO SQL in 1988. Since then ANSI/ISO SQL regular carried on to evolve. The ANSI-SQL team has since posted 3 requirements with the years:

SQL is a query language. It's Easy and english-like to work with. Nevertheless, although there tend to be more than ninety SQL reserved words, nearly all programmers seldom use much more than the following couple of commands - SELECT, ORDER, IN,

NOT, AND, OR, LIKE, BETWEEN, HAVING, WHERE, FROM, DELETE, UPDATE, INSERT, Group and also BY.

For instance, in case you had a database table called "employees" and also you wanted to retrieve all data in which the employee has got the last title "goodman", you will make use of the following SQL statement:

Select * From workers Where lastname =' goodman'; You will find many distinct types of SQL claims though the standard versions that most programmers must be accustomed to will be the SQL statements.

SQL is predominantly utilized by two kinds of owners - humans and programs (keying in the instructions by way of a database client) - to successfully pass directions to databases. SQL instructions could be keyed right into a database customer including the MySQL Query Browser or the SQL Server Enterprise Manager and carried out to sometimes go back an outcome or change data in the website.

SQL may additionally be utilized and programming language or scripting language as Microsoft Visual Basic and PHP to speak with the database. Although SQL is a planet standard format, it's regrettable that many data source vendors have developed various variations and dialects.

This is because every database vendor wishes to differentiate their database products from the crowd. A great example is Microsoft SQL Server's TRANSACT SQL. TRANSACT SQL is a superset of SQL and it is created for use just with Microsoft SQL Server.

Though it does make programming much simpler for software developers, it's not compliant with different databases as Mysql or Oracle - creating TRANSACT SQL applications non database portable.

As a result, although a number of these characteristics are robust and powerful, it is good practice to exercise extreme caution and control your SQL use to become compliant with the ANSI/ISO SQL requirements and ODBC Compliant.

This is a complete introductory guide on SQL for beginners. I hope you'll make the best use of it.

Let's get started

CHAPTER 1

What Is SQL?

SQL stands for Structured Query Language and it is a declarative programming vocabulary utilized to access and manipulate information in RDBMS (Relational Database Management Systems). SQL was created by IBM in 70's for their major platform.

Over the years, SQL started to be standardized by equally American National Standards Institute (International Organization and ansi-sql) for Standardization (ISO SQL). Based on ANSI SQL is pronounced "es queue el", most software program and repository developers with history in MS SQL Server pronounce it "sequel".

A Relational Database Management System is a portion of a program utilized to store and control information in database items known as tables. A relational database table is a tabular information system placed in rows and columns.

The table columns likewise referred to as table fields have different attributes and unique names defining the column sort, default worth, indexes and many other column characteristics. The relational data source table rows is the real information entries.

The most used RDBMS are Oracle from Oracle Corp., MySQL from MySQL, MS SQL Server from Microsoft, DB2 from IBM, and MS

Access from Microsoft. Many business data source vendors have created the proprietary SQL extension based on ANSI SQL standard.

For instance the SQL edition employed by MS SQL Server is known as T SQL or Transact SQL, The Oracle's model is known as PL/SQL - Procedural Language/SQL), and MS Access utilize Jet SQL.

SQL queries are utilized to access information from repository tables. The SQL queries utilize the SELECT SQL key phrase that is an element of the (DQL) Data Query Language. If we've a table named "Orders" and also you are looking to pick all entries in which the purchase great is in excess of hundred dollars ordered by the order worth, you can get it done with the following SQL SELECT query:

SELECT OrderID, OrderDate, CustomerID, ProductID, OrderValue

From Orders
Wherever OrderValue andgt; 200

Order BY OrderValue;

The From SQL clause instructs from which table(s) we are retrieving information. The Where SQL clause says search criteria (in our case to access just data with OrderValue better than 1dolar1 200). The Order BY clause instructs the returned information must be purchase by the OrderValue column. The Where and Order BY clauses are suggested.

You can manipulate information kept in relational data source tables, by utilizing the INSERT, Update and DELETE SQL keyword phrases. These 3 SQL instructions are included in the information Manipulation Language (DML).

-- In order to insert data to a table named "Orders" you can work with a SQL statement much like the main below:

INSERT Into Orders (ProductID, OrderValue OrderDate, CustomerID,)

VALUES (ten, hundred eight,' 12/12/2007', 99.95);

-- In order to modify details in a table you can utilize a statement as this:

Upgrade Orders

Set OrderValue = 199.99

Wherever CustomerID = ten And OrderDate =' 12/12/2007';

-- In order to delete information from database table utilize a statement such as the one below:

DELETE Orders

Wherever CustomerID = ten; You can create, change and delete database items (example of database items are data source tables, views, saved methods, etc.), by getting the CREATE, Alter and Drop SQL keyword phrases. These 3 SQL keywords are included in the information Definition Language (DDL). For instance to produce table "Orders" you can make use of the SQL statement:

Make Orders

(OrderID INT IDENTITY(1, 1) PRIMARY KEY,

CustomerID ID,

ProductID INT,

OrderValue Currency

OrderDate DATE,

You can also manage database items privileges by utilizing the GRANT and also REVOKE keywords, with (DCL) the information Control Language. For instance to enable the person with "User1" as the username to choose information from the table "Orders" you can make use of the SQL statement:

GRANT SELECT ON Orders TO User1

Today every program professional needs a minimum of a simple understanding of how SQL functions. In case you are new to SQL, you may feel confused and confused in the novice, but as you advance you will discover how elegant and powerful SQL is.

CHAPTER 2

Why Is SQL Important?

Network programs are larger and more flexible. In many cases, the fundamental scheme of operations is mainly a mix of scripts that handle the command of a database.

Due to the variety of languages and pre-existing sources, the method to "talk" between one another may usually be challenging and complicated, fortunately for us, the presence of requirements that permit us to do the typical methods by way of a wide spread form can make this particular perplexing task even more simple.

That is what Structured Query Language (SQL) is based on, that typically is only a worldwide common language of interaction within databases. That is precisely why, the Structured Query Language (SQL) is really a standardized language which allows most people to apply some language e.g. PHP or ASP, in conjunction with any particular database e.g. MySQL, MS Access, SQL Server.

SQL was made by IBM throughout the1970's; in the novice it had been named SEQUEL (Structure English Query Language). Years later, Oracle and Microsoft also began with the use of SEQUEL.

The global recognition grew after which the word SEQUEL was transformed. In 1986, the word SEQUEL was standardized by the American National Standards Institute (ANSI) to SQL. In other words, they ditched the earth "English" from the word.

Until this morning, there are plenty of owners that decline to reference it as SQL, to these individuals; SEQUEL definitely may be the proper rap because of this standardized data source language. SQL has also been revised in 1989 and 1992. Since then, SQL has undergone a lot of revisions to improve their standardization.

SQL is certainly a worldwide standardized vocabulary, but that doesn't imply that is very similar for every repository. Truth be told, many databases execute particular functions which won't generally run in others.

That is the explanation why every business that gives database solutions, for example Oracle and Microsoft, have their own certification process ensuring that people who takes the certification examination are really well prepared and understand the differences in between the different types of SQL. Their knowledge is concentrating on their own distinctive certain variant of SQL.

SQL isn't simply relevant due to the ability to standardize a usually confusing language; it offers two other special characteristics. On a single hand, it actually is tremendously adaptable and powerful. On the opposite hand, it's really accessible which makes it much easier to master.

There are lots of databases items that support SQL, nonetheless, two of the largest and most popular are Microsoft SQL server and Oracle website.

Each company that provides database product has their own path to be an "expert". For instance, Microsoft offers an assortment of accreditation to guarantee that each Microsoft SQL Certified meets their criteria. Oracle does exactly the same thing with their Certification process.

CHAPTER 3

What Is SQL Web Hosting?

SQL is the acronym or light for Structured Query Language. SQL is needed managing information in a specific database. So why do we have to have knowledge concerning SQL?

Mainly because the sites as we realize it wouldn't work without this language.

The language was created for IBM and has radically transformed the face of net designing and information management. With all the usage of SQL large amount of information may be managed very easily with no hassle and it's turned out to be the language of preference for nearly all individuals in this particular area.

SQL has developed with time to suit many operating systems and today you will find many types or SQL committed for different operating systems as windows, Mac or Linux.

Relational Database Management Systems or RDBMS as we realize it wouldn't have existed with no SQL. The structured Query Language provides a really easy tactic and therefore it's become an essential component of net structuring and management.

The primary benefit of Structures Query Language is that the quantity of information being managed can differ though the fundamental framework is still similar hence the same platform is often utilized for tiny sites handling a handful of appointments one day to large sites handling visitors of as much as countless visits one day.

If your website handles a lot of traffic and it's perfectly necessary to keep it running efficiently on a regular basis next SQL is the best choice for you. 4

With SQL you can handle the system and tremendous load won't flinch still beyond peak capacity. With Structured Query Language you can additionally perform routine maintenance job of your website without compromising the performance of the website.

SQL web hosting has various advantages which win more than some other types of web hosting. Foremost it's a really rapid and cost effective method of handling a site.

SQL Web Hosts also offers toolbars that will aid you have a tab on the exercise on your site and check views. The Hosts will additionally provide feedback on the running of your site like pro opinions on the viability of your site.

But if your company cannot afford a separate IT wing next SQL web hosts will additionally help structure your site based on your needs and additionally recommend Hosting Plans particularly designed for your requirements and also the comfort of your customers.

On the flip side in case your company can manage to use IT engineers then you can simply employ servers and employ SQL to your advantage as you deem healthy.

With all the use of SQL, you receive higher speed and the ability to perform tasks as maintenance and renovation of your website better. Thus this vocabulary has turned out to be the language Web Hosting market.

The benefits of SQL are many but on the downside the establishment price and operating costs are rather substantial. SQL is beyond the access of little and medium businesses. An additional disadvantage is the fact that you can find particular versions for precise operating systems so it gets hard of many os's are installed in your device.

SQL web hosting is a program which enables SQL directories to be hosted on the web. SQL web hosting may be utilized to hold database info on the internet, permit offsite private to make use of database management programs and also give comprehensive info to clients or customers.

Common applications which use SQL databases are Enterprise Resource Planning - ERP and Customer Relationship Management - CRM applications.

What exactly are the Advantages of SQL Web Hosting?

There are many good things about purchasing an SQL web hosting service instead of depending on a regular web host. If perhaps you need an online database, you'll rapidly come to value these benefits

Enhanced Bandwidth and RAM - Typically, database programs take up a lot of mind and server space. SQL web hosting services offer extra room for the database to develop and grow over time.

Administration Services of SQL - web hosting services of SQL are devoted to database hosting, they usually have the capacity to provide superior administration offerings to always keep your database running efficiently and at maximum overall performance.

Technical SQL and Assistance Design - If you are a novice to SQL, many SQL web hosting services offer technical assistance and design bundles for an extra price whenever you buy web hosting.

Issues to Search for in an excellent SQL Web Hosting Service Once you have chosen to choose an SQL web host, you will have to pick a service. You will find a lot of providers already on the market, and often it is hard to inform them apart. A quality SQL web hosting service can provide you with the following:

Reliability

Control Panel Options

Complex Support

Buyer Support

Many Hosting Plans

General, in case you intend on keeping a database online, your best option is going with a web hosting service which has servers dedicated especially to SQL uses.

Doing this will ensure you receive the best value out of your investment. SQL web hosting may cost you a bit more than regular hosting, though it is worth every penny.

CHAPTER 4

What Is SQL Injection?

SQL Injection is among the countless web encounter mechanisms utilized by hackers to steal information from organizations. It's possibly the most popular application layer attack methods used now.

Web applications enable genuine site visitors to retrieve and submit details to/from a database with the web using the choice web browser.

Databases are likewise central to contemporary sites - they save information required for sites to provide particular information to guests and render info to clients, suppliers, workers and a multitude of stakeholders.

User credentials, financial and payment info, business data might all be resident in just a database and seen by genuine people via off-the-shelf and customized web apps. Databases and web applications allow you to routinely run your business.

SQL Injection will be the hacking method that tries to pass SQL instructions by way of a web program for delivery by the backend database. If it wasn't sanitized correctly, web applications might lead to SQL Injection attacks that enable hackers to look at info from the database and/or actually wipe it out.

This kind of characteristics as login webpages, help and item request forms, feedback styles, search webpages, shopping carts and the normal delivery of compelling content, shape contemporary sites and supply companies with the means important to speak with customers and prospects. These site functions tend to be examples of web apps which might be often purchased off-the-shelf or produced as bespoke shows.

These site features are all prone to SQL Injection attacks.

SQL Injection: An Example

Take an easy login page in which a respectable user would enter his username and password combination to enter a protected place to view his personal details or upload his comments in a forum.

If a real user submits his details,SQL query is generated out of these details and submitted to the database for verification. If legitimate, the person is allowed access.

Put simply, the net program which regulates the login page will speak with the database by way of a number of planned commands and so as to confirm the username and password mixture. On verification, the genuine user is granted proper access.

Through SQL Injection, the hacker might enter particularly crafted SQL instructions with the intention of bypassing the login form screen and seeing what is behind it. This is only likely in case the inputs aren't correctly sanitized (i.e., made invulnerable) and delivered straight with the SQL query on the website. SQL Injection vulnerabilities supply the means for a hacker to talk straight to the website.

The technologies susceptible to this particular attack are powerful software languages like ASP.NET, PHP, ASP, JSP, and also CGI. All an assailant must do an SQL Injection hacking episode is an internet browser, awareness of Creative guess and sql queries work to essential field and table labels.

Precisely why can it be easy to pass SQL queries straight to a database that is concealed behind a firewall and other protection mechanism?

Firewalls and related intrusion detection mechanisms present small or no defense against full scale SQL Injection net attacks.

Because your website has to be public, protection mechanisms will allow public web visitors to speak with your net application/s (generally over port 80/443). The net application has open a chance to access the website to be able to go back (update) the requested (changed) info.

Inside SQL Injection, the hacker utilizes SQL queries and imagination to reach the database of sensitive company details with the net program.

SQL or Structured Query Language could be the computer language which enables you to save, control, and access information kept in a relational database (or a group of tables that organise and structure information).

SQL is, actually, the one way that a web program (and users) may communicate with the database. Types of relational databases consist of Microsoft Access, Oracle, MySQL, MS SQL Server, and Filemaker Pro, every one of what use SQL as the building blocks.

The SQL commands include INSERT, SELECT, Drop and Delete TABLE.

The Drop Table is ominous as it may sound and actually will get rid of the table with a specific title.

In the respectable situation of the login page example earlier, the SQL commands designed for the net application program might be as the following:

Choose count(*)

Wherever username='FIELD_USERNAME'

From users_list_table

And password='FIELD_PASSWORD"

In simple English, SQL command (from the net application) teaches the database to complement the username and password enter by the respectable user on the mixture it's already saved.

Each web application is coded with particular SQL queries that will be executed when performing legitimate roles and talking with the database. If any input industry of the net application isn't correctly sanitized, a hacker might inject extra SQL commands which broaden the assortment of SQL commands the net application will execute, therefore going beyond the initial planned function and design.

A hacker will therefore have a specific channel of interaction to the database regardless of all of the community security equipment fitted and intrusion detection systems prior to the bodily data source server.

Is the database vulnerable to SQL Injection?

SQL Injection is among the most typical application layer attacks presently being used on the web. Regardless of the reality that it's reasonably simple to guard against SQL Injection, you will find a lot of web apps that will remain weak.

Based on the net Application Security Consortium (WASC) nine % of the entire hacking incidents reported in the press until 27th July

2006 were because of SQL Injection. Newer information from our research suggests that approximately fifty % of the sites we've scanned the season are vulnerable to SQL Injection vulnerabilities.

It may be tough to reply to the question whether your web site and web applications are susceptible to SQL Injection particularly in case you are not a coder or you are not the individual who has coded your web applications.

Our experience leads us to think that there's a tremendous possibility that your data has already been vulnerable from SQL Injection.

Whether an assailant has the ability to see the information saved on the database or otherwise, truly depends on how your website is coded to show the outcomes of the queries sent. What's specific is that the assailant will be ready in order to perform arbitrary SQL Commands on the weak phone system, sometimes to compromise it otherwise to get info.

If improperly coded, then you definitely run the danger of having your customer and company data compromised.

When an attacker gains access to additionally is dependent on the amount of protection established by the website. The database might be set to restrict to particular commands only. A read access usually is enabled to be used by web program back stops.

Even when an assailant can't modify the system, he would still have the ability to read valuable information.

What's the effect of SQL Injection?

When an assailant knows that a device is susceptible to SQL Injection, he's in a position to inject SQL Query / Commands with an input type area. This is the same as handing the attacker of your database and permitting him to perform some SQL command such as Drop Table on the database!

An assailant might execute arbitrary SQL claims on the weak phone system. This might compromise the integrity of your database and/or expose sensitive info.

Determined by the back end data source of use, SQL injection vulnerabilities result in different degrees of data/system access for the enemy. It might be easy to adjust pre-existing queries, to UNION (used to choose associated info from 2 tables) arbitrary details, utilize subselects, or tack extra queries.

In many instances, it can be feasible in order to check out in and create away to documents, and to perform layer instructions on the basic operating system.[break][break]Certain SQL Servers like Microsoft SQL Server have saved and extended methods (database server functions). If an assailant can get access to these methods it

Sadly the effect of SQL Injection is just uncovered once the theft is discovered. Data has been unwittingly stolen through different hack attacks all of the time. The greater number of specialist of hackers seldom gets caught.

Example of a SQL Injection Attack Here's a sample simple HTML type with 2 inputs, password and login.

http://testasp.acunetix.com/login.asp"andgt;

The simplest way for the login.asp to do the job is actually by creating a collection query which seems as this:

Choose id

From logins

Wherever username =' 1dolar1 username'

And password =' 1dolar1 password' If the variables 1 username and 1 password are requested from the user's feedback, this could effortlessly be affected. Assume we provided "Joe" as a username which the next string was offered as a password: anything' Or' x'='x

Choose id

From logins

Wherever username =' Joe'

And password =' anything' Or' x'='x' As the inputs of the net program aren't correctly sanitized, the usage of the one quotes has transformed the Where SQL command into a two component clause.

The' x'='x' component promises to be true no matter how much the first component has.

This can enable the assailant to avoid the login form without truly understanding a legitimate username / password mixture!

Firewalls and related intrusion detection mechanisms provide minimal defense against full scale web attacks. Because your website must be public, the security mechanisms will enable public web visitors to speak with your private databases servers via web apps. Is not this what they have been created to do?

Patching your databases, servers, programming languages and os's is vital but is not the simplest way to avoid SQL Injection Attacks.

CHAPTER 5

What Is a SQL Injection Attack?

Owners of site visitors and computer systems are acquainted with proving and authenticating their identity, "they are the person they claim they are," by putting in their Password and Username.

What really happens if you get into copy into the Password and Username areas of a login display is that the book is generally placed or encapsulated right into SQL command.

Sql command checks the information you have entered in contrary to the info kept in the database, like user names and passwords. If the input matches what's kept in the database then you are granted a chance to access the product. If it wasn't, you receive an error message and an opportunity to reenter the appropriate info or you are refused completely.

Databases are at the center of a contemporary organization's computer systems since they enable you to control your business processes. They save data needed to provide certain content to visitors, suppliers, customers, and staff.

User credentials, payment information, financials, and organization statistics may all reside in just a database that may be accessed by genuine users and regrettably attackers also. SQL and/or

Structured Query Language could be the computer language which enables you to save, control, and access information kept in the database

SQL injection is also the exploitation of a site or computer which is brought on through the processing of invalid information which is imputed into the type fields by a computer user that is malicious. SQL injection could be utilized by an attacker to expose (or "inject") code into a laptop program to alter the course of execution to be able to access and control the database behind the website, application or system.

SQL Injection vulnerabilities develop because the fields for consumer input allow SQL statements to pass through to the database straight to be able to process information and operator requests. In case the input isn't filtered correctly, web applications might enable SQL commands which enable hackers to open unauthorized info from the database or wipe it out.

The strike takes advantage of incorrect coding of web based programs and computer networks which incorporates functions that provide dynamic content this kind of as:

Login pages

Item demand forms

Client assistance pages

Responses forms

Search pages

Shopping carts If the genuine user submits his details, a SQL query is produced out of these details and posted to the database for verification. Utilizing SQL Injection, the hacker might enter particularly crafted SQL instructions with the intention of bypassing the type screen and seeing what is behind it.

Often each an assailant must do a SQL Injection hacking episode is an internet browser, awareness of SQL queries, moreover imagination to imagine crucial field and table names.

An illustration of SQL injection attack is as follows;

An assailant attempts at compromising a method which they have absolutely no permission to access by entering code rather than their credentials.

When the assailant is caused to get into their Password and Username he goes into codes like as' x'='x'. And based the way the system's program is written, this particular command will be true because x often equal x, therefore the Password and Username combination will invariably be true or match!

When an attacker realizes that a device is susceptible to SQL Injection, he's in a position to inject SQL Commands with the input area. This enables the assailant to perform some SQL command on the website, copying, including modifying, and also deleting information.

Detect SQL Injection Attacks

With all the growing up of B/S design program development, an increasing number of coder write plan with it. Sadly, a lot of programmers didn't determine the validity of users' enter information during encoding, and next, there'll be security danger in the program.

Malicious attackers publish a unique segment of repository query code on the server, the server will disclosure some very sensitive info when respond with corresponding consequence. This is SQL Injection Attack.

The primary pattern Firewall presently won't alarm when there's SQL encounter due to the SQL Injection is through regular point and difficult and hidden to be detected, apparently regular site visit.

The risk of SQL Injection Attack Based on the data of CVE in 2006, there tends to be more than seventy % attacks dependent on web program. The SQL Injection Attack improve year by year, it comes at 1078 in 2006. Although, these information is just for the vulnerability in common uses currently.

The risk of Attack including: Change the information in database with no authorization.

Acquire the administration authority of a website with no authorization.

Maliciously change content of a website with no authorization.

XSS attacks.

Gain the management authority of the server with no authorization.

Add, delete and alter the accounts in the server with no authorization.

The procedure for identify and revert Attack with Sax2 Some IDS programs will perform good detection for SQL Injection Attack, although, firewall cannot. Let's visit the procedure of identify and revert SQL Injection Attack with IDS application Sax2.

The steps of Attack are:

Determine setting to search for the injection point.

Determine the kind of website.

Guess the content.

Guess datasheet.

Guess the industry.

The measures "Guess datasheet", "Guess the field" and "Guess the content" are really crucial for SQL Injection Attack while in the total procedure.

The assailant will determine the length of the filed and imagine the information after discovered the corresponding submitted. It will be a strike following the attacker guess the information in the filed effectively. Often, the assailant must decryption the information in case it in MD5 encryption.

Above will be the entire process of SQL Injection Attack and also we detect it with Sax2. We all know that, Sax2 may efficiently identify and alarm the Attack when it happens. IDS program Sax2 is a helpful tool for Attack and make your network security combine with firewall application.

CHAPTER 6

The Best Way To Prevent Sql Injection Attacks

SQL Injection attacks could cripple your web site in case you are not cautious. I am going to suggest various ways to prevent them when working with PHP/MySQL. I have heard of many different remedies coming from different people and even many of them are extremely ineffective - you will understand why.

Establishing Maxlength

The first method I will discuss is ineffective but is usually recommended. That is establishing a maxlength on an input area to disallow owners from getting into lengthy intricate SQL injection attacks.

Establishing the maxlength feature on an HTML input area is only a tiny obstacle which may easily be circumvented. In reality, something that is customer side isn't an answer but simply an inconvenience for an intruder.

Cap Permissions

The database user you utilize to connect to your database shouldn't be set as the best level administrator. Rather, produce a new user which contains just the permissions needed by your web site.

For instance, if the front end of your website just reads details from the database and then hook up to the collection with an account that just has SELECT permissions. This method is indeed helpful, but with a good attack, an intruder can create their superuser from an easy SELECT statement too.

Switch on Magic Quotes Turn on magic quotes in your PHP server options (that is the magic_quotes_gpc variable). What this does is instantly escape quotes and other specific characters with a backslash; in that way SQL will not identify the quote together with the query and cure it the same as every other character.

This is instantly completed for any HTTP request information like Post, Get and also COOKIE. Because it just cleans HTTP request information, secret quotes stops so but only a few SQL injection attacks!

Information passed into SQL statements coming from the database or files isn't filtered and therefore could be manipulated to be an SQL injection attack based on how your site utilizes this data.

Nevertheless, this is probably the best solution for newbies. It is "set it and forget about it" since all of the tasks are completed for you immediately. Regrettably, if for whatever reason magic quotes becomes turned off (a chance with managed hosting/shared hosting), your website is suddenly in danger for an SQL injection attack.

This is why you should constantly do many of your personal dirty work

Do your Input Cleaning Since you can never ever be certain that magic quotes will remain on, you should actually clean up submitted data yourself.

This is often accomplished by examining whether magic quotes is on with the get_magic_quotes_gpc() command. In case it returns incorrect, you can escape special characters and quotes by hand with the easy addslashes command. It will look a bit something as this:

```
$username = $_POST['username'];

$password = $_POST['password'];

if (!get_magic_quotes_gpc()) {

$username = addslashes($username);

$password = addslashes($password);

}
```

Yet another technique is assuming magic quotes is definitely off and also do your cleaning for everything.Harry Fuecks from

SitePoint developed this small piece of code to remove some slashes included by secret quotes in case it's on. By doing this you have an assurance that all information you are working with is untouched by secret quotes.

```
if (get_magic_quotes_gpc()) {

$_REQUEST = array_map('stripslashes', $_REQUEST);

$_GET = array_map('stripslashes', $_GET);

$_POST = array_map('stripslashes', $_POST);

$_COOKIE = array_map('stripslashes', $_COOKIE); }
```

The very best method of all is a mix of all of the remedies above. If nothing, be sure you comprehend how magic quotes go rather than merely taking it for granted since one day it'll get turned off and you will be screwed!

Magic quotes is your friend but keep in mind, it does not stop each SQL injection attacks. So to be truly secure, it's best to do your cleaning, assuming you get it done correctly!

One of the more successful ways of stopping SQL injection from being utilized is to completely validate each enter from the person, by determining all possible meta characters that may be used by the database process and also filtering them out.

Filters must stay in place to remove all but recognized excellent information. An account lockout policy must additionally be in position to stop the brute force wondering of passwords.

Most validation for security reasons should be performed inside the server side script without comprehensive customer side authentication - for example JavaScript - because it can effortlessly be bypassed by the person disabling JavaScript in their browser.

When working with a numeric feedback, like age, telephone number or credit/debit card number the valuation of the variable really should be prepared by way of a uniquely built purpose to make sure that the information just includes numeric characters (and potentially spaces).

Identical features could be built to deal with various other details variations like Dates, Integers and Floats. Conversely, for many numeric fields such as for instance integers and dates the input strategy might be via the usage of a drop down choice box. In case the input is selected out of a dropdown box it will be produced by the source code and no validation will be essential.

When coping with string inputs it might be required on some occasions to enable the use of certain meta-characters. As a good example, the tick must be permitted to be utilized in the surname filed simply names like O'Conner are accepted.

In this instance it will be better to acknowledge the title and change the apostrophe with two apostrophes prior to operating it through the query or entering it in the website.

When working with all person inputs via text boxes, it's essential to limit the length of the feedback. All textbox fields must be as short as you can and should be a suitable length for the information to be entered. By maintaining every arena as light as they can, the amount of characters that an attacker would use to release a SQL injection is restricted.

One particular type of defense are the Restriction of Error Messages. Error messages are usually produced in HTML which an assailant will have the ability to view. The specifics of all error messages must be logged in file or database on the server and shown by way of a dynamically created error page.

For every query performed to the code of the application program, probably the most limited access rights possible must be due to the query itself. As a good example, the information from a username and password text box holding a login page must be merely applied to a query set up with code which ensures' read only' permissions are provided. This will stop the attacker from inserting data to the database from the written text box.

Stored procedures are an enhanced feature provided by many SQL servers. And supplying a little protection from SQL injection the usage of saved methods additionally boosts the functionality of the site by permitting the net program to compile and run SQL claims in the server itself.

When stored methods are utilized a selection of problems has to be greeted by the injected code to become effective; the malicious SQL should be in specified organized format, with the appropriate amount of details to achieve success. The number and structure of parameters can vary tremendously upon based upon programming choices made by the net developer.

To evaluate a site against an attack it's not needed to become an authority at SQL injection because there are much application based automatic resources offered - like the Web Vulnerability Scanner by Soatest and Acunetix by Parasoft - that can be utilized to systematically do a selection of attacks against and SQL Injection. Automated testing must be performed on a frequent basis and after any significant changes to the web site or server.

SQL Injection attacks provide a major risk to the security of powerful web sites and it's crucial that satisfactory countermeasures are taken to avoid such an assault by achieving success.

Theoretically, if meta-characters have been handled hundred % efficiently the danger of this attack type through web browser types will be eliminated. In truth - in the event that this was the sole type of defence - it will be incredibly simple for a programming error to be produced making the system vulnerable.

The most effective way is taking as many precautions as likely; this is referred to as the' defense of depth' idea. A mix of protection measures such as; validation, neutralizing or meta characters, limiting limiting access and error messages rights to the net server could be utilized to adequately defend an internet base program against a SQL injection attack.

This particular technique and comprehensive assessment as among the last phases of web development, combined with consistent security and testing evaluations must be adequate to safeguard against this SQL injection.

CHAPTER 7

Composing SQL Statements - Tips And Tricks For The Beginner

Assuming you are not a seasoned coder and also know just enough about SQL making you extremely interesting about understanding more often, these ideas and techniques for any SQL beginner might assist you in your latest SQL project.

Assuming you understand many of the fundamentals of composing SQL queries, these suggestions can alleviate many of your struggles with obtaining the query results you are truly searching for.

Fundamental query explanations

Select * From table_name Where Name Like' rd' The benefits can have all items which have a title which ends in card. The % indication is definitely the wild card and also may be set before a word or a part of a word, after the term or before and after a word. Therefore in case you wish to show all products which are cards, this are available in handy.

Incorporating modifiers in your SQL statement

Select * From table_name Where Name Like' %Disney %'

And Name Like' %label %'; Suppose you would like showing all items which are Disney items and are standard address labels. You will use the above mentioned SQL statement.

Using And many times in a single query

Select * From table_name Where Name' rd %'

And Name' %label %'

And Company='Checks To Go'

And Price Using and also to get much more certain results

And may additionally be utilized to get more comprehensive info and it is often followed

by (column1='widgetgreen' or column2='widgetblue' or column3='widgetpink')

And (column1='card' or column2='boohaahaas' or column3='minihahas')

The statement may look as this:

Select * From table_name Where Name' rd %'

AND

(column1='widgetgreen'

or column2='widgetblue'

or column3='widgetpink')

AND

(column1='card'

or column2='boohaahaas'

or column3='minihahas'

); Getting restricted results with SQL statements can help your website start to be simple to navigate and find the merchandise your customers are searching for. This particular info will help anybody starting to discover how you can create SQL statements produce better site articles.

Compelling SQL STATEMENTS

Dynamic SQL claims are SQL claims which are built dynamically from a calling plan.

For instance let us consider the situation of an application in Visual Basic containing an ADO link to a MS ACCESS website.

The ADO link item subsequently utilizes a SQL execute statement, that needs a SQL statement as one inputs and also has a record status adjustable to show whether the query has returned a not discovered and has returned identical data. Normally the SQL statement will be one that serves a certain purpose like displaying a summary of employee names.

Select Emp_Name from Emp_Master.

And the above mentioned query suppose you have a type area which takes Dept_No and Emp_No as inputs on the form and passes it with the calling plan. So now we want to select a worker with a certain employee number or a worker with a certain department number.

So we want a query that is dynamic and which relates to either a certain employee number or department number.

And so the exact same query used above will show up as

Select Emp_Name from Emp_Master just where emp_id = "'andEmp_Noand"""

Here the Emp_No is transferred out of the calling plan and it is concatenated to the primary query dynamically utilizing "'andEmp_Noand"""

The query will appear as Select Emp_Name from Emp_Master just where emp_id =' E001' or in the case where' E004' is transferred out of the key type the query will dynamically transform to pick Emp_Name from Emp_Master where emp_id =' E004'.

In the situation when department quantity is passed out of the key system the query will be coded as

Select Emp_Name from Emp_Master wherein dept_name = andamp; "" anddept_nameand"" where andamp; is the concatenation operator So dynamically when D002 is passed as a variable out of the key system the query will appear as Select Emp_Name from Emp_Master where dept_name ='D002'.

The ADO.Execute declaration (Used for performing a SQL statement in an ADO connection will appear as ADO.Execute("Select Emp_Name from Emp_Master wherein dept_name =' D002'), earlier the ADO.Execute would have just Static SQL statements. Right here there might be far more techniques apart from ADO used to link an external system to the database

Utilizing compelling SQL one may code exactly where clauses, SQL statements, pass table labels. The sole disadvantage of utilizing dynamic SQL is that the statements aren't compiled just before run time which could cause performance degradation.

CHAPTER 8

Punctuation In SQL - When You Should Use Semi-Colons And Commas Within Microsoft's Transact SQL/T-SQL

Assume you are attempting to get info from an SQL Server table by using SQL Server. The table is known as tblPerson, and also has 2 fields: First LastName and Name. This artilce explains if you will use punctuation and once you would not.

Semi-Colons

The semi colon character (;) is elective in the conclusion of instructions. For instance, the following command is acceptable:

SELECT

[First Name],

LastName

FROM

tblPerson;

On the other hand, therefore is this:

SELECT

[First Name],

LastName

FROM

tblPerson You might think it is helpful to establish whenever a command has completed, but the SQL compiler does not require you to accomplish this. Me personally, the writer would not bother with semi-colons.

Commas

You make use of commas (, to distinguish columns, even if in a SELECT clause or in an Order BY clause. For example:

SELECT

[First Name], LastName

FROM

tblPerson

Purchase BY

LastName, FirstName

You have to place a comma after each column at a summary aside from the previous one. Some people like to place the comma at the beginning of every line - like this:

SELECT

[First Name]

,LastName

FROM

tblPerson The benefit of this approach is the fact that you can delete and put lines without it impacting the sense of your command. For the writer this is a little too techie!

Square Brackets

You make use of square brackets round table and area names: optionally, when the names do not have areas in, and compulsorily if not. For example:

SELECT

[First Name],

[LastName]

FROM

[tblPerson] In this particular instance, the square brackets round the FirstName column are required (though you can utilize individual quotation marks instead); the people round the LastName column and tblPerson table title are not needed, even though they are not performing any damage.

Round Brackets

You make use of round brackets in SQL to present or finish a characteristic call, the same as in Excel. For example:

SELECT

Len([First Name]) AS [First title length],

LastName

FROM

tblPerson Here the brackets after the Len feature enclose the summary of debates (the pieces of info it requires to be able to work).

CHAPTER 9

The Order Of Commands In SQL

The issue - is writing T SQL, SFWGHO Microsoft's takes the SQL database language, the instructions need to are available in a particular order. This particular is:

- (selecting data)SELECT

- (stating what table to become information from)From

- (any filtering conditions)Where

- (specifying some aggregation to perform)Group BY

- (any filtering to operate on aggregated data)Having

- (which order to show the last rows in) Order BY

It's essential you place these instructions in the proper order, or else you will receive a syntax error. The acronym for the instructions is SFWGHO, therefore it is actually only a question of locating a method to recall the sequence of letters.

Solutions

I discovered a single website that had been running a competition, with a single entrant:

Slippery Fish Will Garnish Hungry Orcas

Certainly there should be much better acronyms than that! A bit of reflection developed the next ideas:

6 Fat Wives Gross Husbands Out

Flushed Feet Can give Horrible Odours

Out of these, the next seems better (it is definitely in improved taste!). And so here's my recommendation for how you can recall the order of commands within SQL:

Select or sweaty

Foot and FROM

WILL or WHERE

Give or Group BY

Terrible or HAVING

ORDER or ODOURS BY Now there is absolutely no justification for obtaining the order of SQL instructions bad, we simply have to discover a means to recall to place commas in the correct spot all of the time..

CHAPTER 10

Ways In Order To Use SQL In Order To Query A Lotto Combination File

Reducing improbable combinations of lotto is the primary objective for most players of lottery. This chapter describes how you can make use of SQL, to identify particular numeric patterns.

Just what does SQL Need to Do With Lotto Calculations?

SQL is a favorite language for querying a database. Let us learn how it can assist with lotto selections.

As a good example, I am making use of the popular Prime lotto process for the combination file. In each type of six numbers there are:

Three also numbers

One non-prime odd

Two primes

You will find 575,586 lines entirely, but many of the combinations may look as this:

1 2 3 8 twelve thirty two

5 11 12 18 twenty one thirty two

Three four ten twelve thirteen thirty three some players believe consecutive balls as "1, 2, 3" are not likely to take place and so seek to eliminate them from selections. You can utilize SQL for file query; at first for line counting with your criteria and after that to make a new series without or with your specified parameters.

You will need to import the file right into a database. For exploring SQL queries you can use a simple desktop program as MS Access which I am discovered is great for as much as approximately 100,000 combinations. We will not be taking a look at how you can use these applications and can instead concentrate on employing the SQL coding.

I am using MS Access because of this example and my table holds the initial 20,000 lotto lines of the top system.

Examples Of utilizing SQL On a Lotto Combinations File

Let's jump into a few easy examples; we can begin with a mixture count using different parameters.

The database structure is merely an individual table comprising six numbers.

Lines with "1,2,3":

Select count(n1) AS Count

From PrimeLottoSystem20k

Where n1 andlt;andgt; one and n2 andlt;andgt; two and n3 andlt;andgt; three; In case you consider the query in terminology of everyday language, it is very easy.

"Please count just how many lines you will find where the first 3 numbers aren't 1,2, or 3."

When I ran that query in Access, it returned a matter of 17,093. That means you will find more than 17,000 combinations that have neither "1,2,3" in the first 20,000 lines

Here is a query to determine the number of lines contain just numbers greater that ten.

Select Count(n1) as count

From PrimeLottoSystem2ok

Wherever n1andgt; ten and n2andgt; ten and n3andgt; ten and n4andgt; ten and n5andgt; ten and n6andgt; ten in my database table, the matter was 0 as the sample information was not big enough to meet up with the parameters.

You can possibly notice that a database program as MS Access is not adequate to handle significant study but is a kick off point for understanding about SQL.

CHAPTER 11

Profitable SQL Server Monitoring

Server monitoring is crucial to preserve secrecy and privacy of company's records. As a great quantity of essential information is kept in the server, therefore it's not really a decision but a compulsion for an IT business owner to use a server monitoring system to stop his sensitive data from simply being found by the prying eyes.

Apart from protecting many layers of your database, a monitoring program additionally ensures inaccessibility of your record to the hackers.

Thinking about the increasing incidence of cybercrimes, it absolutely provides you with a reassurance that your important database is outside of the access of the cyber goons. It's the context whereby SQL server monitor claims a deserving mention.

An Introduction

An excellent SQL server monitor program should have the requisite characteristics which work to the benefit associated with a corporate structure. While purchasing monitoring program, ensure it caters to your requirements and offers the actual time transaction stats.

Applications Manager SQL monitoring program is of help that is great for the database administrators so far as performance monitoring is involved. Being an agent less monitoring remedy, it offers unmatched performance metrics to make certain that your SQL server runs efficiently and smoothly.

Getting on the Chore: Applications supervisor manages a lot which speaks volume for its out-of-the-pattern performance. The net customer of the program supervisor plays a tremendous role by assisting you to envisage and also manage MSSQL server database.

The web client additionally provides in-depth and in-detail data monitor. This particular function can help you make an educated choice concerning strategy capability, usage design and make a warning signal in the event of impending issues.

And today there's the Real cause Analysis that provides its helping hand on the server database administrator for the objective of troubleshooting the performance difficulties.

The' Grouping Capability' is an add on element that can help to assemble a database on the foundation of supported company methods. Such a facility allows the operations staff to connect priority to the received sensors.

SQL Server Monitoring More to Offer:

SQL server can juggle many hats at exactly the same point of time. It's fitted with a few practical capabilities that can linking to the database source and monitor varied method table column values. Notification and data collection by using sensors can also be handled by the SQL monitor plan.

Memory consumption, database details, cache details, relationship data and SQ figures are a number of key elements that are taken great proper care of in SQL database as a component of the monitoring program.

Extra proposal for the SQL server software users monitoring – The Applications Manager utilizes the Query Monitoring capability of the database to monitor SQL Query of MS SQL database. With the trength of this added element, a database administrator can monitor additional performance and custom database matrices.

Additionally, this extra offering can present Business Metrics to Line of Business Managers. As protection is your top priority, therefore you'll certainly not mind spending a bit of additional for a profitable SQL server monitor program.

CHAPTER 12

What Exactly Are The Advantages Of An SQL Hosting Service?

When you are in the system of getting a company site for your company, you might have to make use of a database. As the title indicates, a database is merely a way for keeping considerable amounts of information in a structured manner.

When you want to add some sort of database with your site, you will find essentially two methods you will begin it: buy an offline database or an online it. By much, the latter is definitely the very best and will be the industry standard so far as database performs in a website is involved.

When you are looking for a means to mix a database with your site, you will realize that you can get many products and standards used out there. Nevertheless, undoubtedly the most typical is using an SQL hosting service.

SQL web hosting ensures you can have your databases online, that also causes it to be easier for elements in your site to access the info contained within them. This is precisely why a lot of the biggest companies work with such solutions to look after their hosting problems.

The other benefit of SQL web hosting is it's really convenient to use. Actually, it could be said to function as the simplest way of performing web hosting while using a database.

The simple fact that many individuals utilize this sort of solution implies that in case you actually run into any issues, you can quickly find either informal or formal support that will help you handle the problem.

Moreover, these kinds of hosting answers are usually fairly adaptable as much as database management is concerned, which means you can utilize it for almost any kind of repository you have under consideration. You don't need to shift to an additional process simply since your database is simply too basic and absurdly complex; the SQL web hosting service is frequently in the position to manage everything.

The other benefit of that web hosting answers is they provide many resources which cause it to be easier for you to be effective. For example, as compared to various other sorts of hosting services, an SQL web host usually presents a lot of bandwidth and memory.

This is typically extremely necessary, given the point that lots of online applications which have to use databases typically need many resources to work. By ensuring you purchase this type of hosting service, you'll greatly make your site much easier to use and manage.

Moreover, many SQL web hosting services also provide unparalleled administration facilities. When you have to utilize a database together with your site, you have to make sure it's stored in order since any mistakes might end up in failure of the whole website.

By benefiting from the administration services in the SQL web hosting service, you can assure you don't need to go through from this kind of issues. These are merely some of the many advantages of utilizing an SQL hosting service with a typical one.

Chapter 13

The Best Way To Manage Your SQL Server Version Control

Just like the weather, SQL coders and database managers discuss version control, but a lot of them don't do anything relating to it. SQL Server Version management suggests managing the versions of the items designed and deployed in their SQL Server environments.

Usually, that requires programmers and DBAs considering scripts including item creation advancement scripts into Visual Source Safe (VSS), or a comparable model management applications, after they create them then checking them away and in again whenever they generate modifications.

Most shops employ version control to make a record of their code - but why don't you think about the database?

To make use of Randolph, you will generally understand your database development is completely versioned, you lose absolutely nothing and can still go back - with practically absolutely no attempt on your part !

You will find a variety of advantages which comes with establishing edition control: one. Command of the versions of items that are used within the various environments

2. Databases object retrieval

3. Change tracking -- detection of deleted or new objects

4. Difference tracking -- detection of what is modified at an object

5. Rationale and Background of object modifications

6. Marking of an edition of database objects to have update scripts

7. Simplified troubleshooting technique by realizing particularly what has changed; and the capability to come again modifications to previous variations of the objects

Remarkably excellent SQL Server Version management software will enable you to perform those activities:

- Full save of the database's entities

- An profitable GUI: Enables an effective searching throughout the database's entities

- Their various attributes, their full background, and also a simple access of each entity's whole source code at each point in time

- Sophisticated reports: Know precisely what occurred on your database across time

- Filtering and looking by means of entities

- Examining Entities - what actually has transformed with every database entity at any point in time

- Integration with SourceSafe, Microsoft Team Foundation and Subversion Server

- Built in scripting engine - Not just the databases: complete monitoring of SQL Server amount entities (Logins, Jobs...)

This particular tool in fact does exist. It changes the responsibility for SQL Server versioning from the owners towards the program.

Its light weight, effortless to work with application which operates to the history and also will keep track of all your databases schema and information adjustments over time, and enables complete evaluation of databases' past, and complete rollback to the point in time, also as optionally push adjustments into pre-existing methods (Subversion, SourceSafe or Team Foundation Server).

CHAPTER 14

Filestream Corruption in SQL - A Phenomenal SQL Database Recovery Solution!

The procedure for saving and controlling unstructured details was inadequate, before SQL Server 2008 release.

Earlier Approaches of Storing Unstructured Data Prior to the release of SQL 2008, there were two methods of storing unstructured information. One method was of storing information in an IMAGE or VARBINARY column. This had transactional consistency and reduced data handling complexities, though it was good performance.

The alternative technique was storing unstructured details as disk documents and also in order to keep the file place in the table together with some structured information connected to it. This approach was helpful in terminology of performance, but didn't ensure transactional consistency.

FILESTREAM Feature - Efficient Storage of Unstructured Data

FILESTREAM feature was unveiled with SQL Server 2008 for storing and controlling unstructured data effectively. This particular function enables saving of BLOB information (like word documents, image files, music file, videos etc) in the NTFS file process. It guarantees transactional consistency in between the unstructured information (stored in NTFS) and the structured information (stored in table).

FILESTREAM Corruption - Error 7904 Sometimes, whenever you attempt to bring MS SQL 2008 data source (MDF files) from transaction log backups, database becomes harmed. You fail to do restoration and hence MDF data start to be unavailable causing data loss.

Exposed to problem that is such, you may face the error: "FILESTREAM crisis - missing documents, mistake 7904." During that time, in case you desire to restore entry of your mission crucial MDF data, you have to complete SQL database healing system utilizing a suitable MDF File Recovery solution.

Initial Database May not Be Corrupted

The database corrupted whenever you attempted to recover the collection from transaction log backups though the initial database, from that the backup of transaction was shot, don't destroys in the majority of the cases. In many of these instances, corruption occurs on the website which was restored from a sequence of backup logs.

The initial data source may not corrupt. "7904 sixteen two Table error: The FILESTRWEAM file for "FileID" wasn't found." You can get back the valuable data with a good SQL Database Recovery

Solution to recuperate corrupt SQL repository contents from corrupt MDF data.

A Phenomenal SQL Database Recovery Solution

SysTools SQL Recovery device is probably the easiest and most effective SQL repository recovery programs offered about. This MDF file healing program performs a considerable scan of broken directories to recover all database products as tables, stored procedures, triggers, forms, reports, etc.

Should you opt to fix SQL DB and also recover corrupt SQL repository by using SysTools SQL Recovery application next you will be gifted with an extremely easy interface that will not demand you to have any previous specialized abilities to perform the SQL healing process.

The application also offers a read only dynamics and that helps you to restore first contents of SQL database. In a nutshell, SysTools SQL Recovery application is a phenomenal SQL Database Recovery Solution.

SysTools Software Group provides intuitive and simple software solutions for data connected needs of users anywhere. The application produced at SysTools are used with technology that is advanced to offer unparalleled outcomes for information recovery, information transformation, and any other such areas covered by SysTools application solutions.

SysTools SQL Recovery device is a remarkable SQL repository recovery formula in order to Open SQL's corrupt MDF data, to repair SQL DB also to recuperate information from all those data.

CHAPTER 15

The Way To Hook Up To An Unresponsive SQL Server Instance: Direct Admin Connection

There might be instances when SQL Server stops answering customer connections though it's still up. This may be a discouraging experience, and also the first impulse is bouncing SQL Server or reboots the server itself. While this might stop the symptom, this particular action will not show you anything that will help you avoid the cause.

For instance, let's state you turn up on Tuesday morning to find out an unresponsive database. The prior night, your developers additional new code on the application servers. Cause or coincidence? With no a means to determine what SQL Server is engaging in, you can't predict. Go into the Direct Admin Connection...

Since SQL SQL Server has got the Direct Admin Connection (DAC) to enable a back door for only such situation.

On the server itself (no system connections unless the remote admins feature was earlier configured), one login that is a part of the sysadmin team can hook up to SQL Server through a DAC to be able to get a concept of what's going on and also have a chance to fix the problem. You will find two techniques to hook up to SQL Server through a DAC.

DAC Method 1

The first technique uses SQLCMD. On the server, wide open a command prompt and enter:

sqlcmd -S localhost -U sa -P password -d master -A You might substitute the sa login with a different login that is a part of the sysadmin group. The A parameter establishes DAC, while the master parameter D tells SQLCMD to use the master database as default because of this session. The master database is certain to be for sale so very long as the example is running, while some other databases might not be publicly available.

DAC Method 2

The next technique uses SSMS. On the server, open the SSMS, then click on ' File' –and ' New' -and;' on the Database Engine Query'. A dialog box shows up (' Connect to the Database Engine'), type' ADMIN :' before the title of the server example.

As a good example, to login through a DAC to example PRODBOULDER, you'd type' ADMIN: PRODBOULDER', now go into the remaining authentication info (remembering to utilize a login together with the sysadmin role), and click' Connect'.

Don't forget, neither of the above will be successful when the login you are utilizing isn't a part of the sysadmin group or if there's an additional DAC now attached to the example.

When associated with either method, you can run queries to identify the root cause of the lock-up. I favor technique #2 above (using SSMS), as I could rapidly access the standard set of queries preserved on the server or paste and copy them from my area machine on the server through my RDP session.

CHAPTER 16

The Best Way To Restore SQL Database Easily With No Difficulty?

MS SQL is an application created by Microsoft that is utilized broadly for effective data management by many businesses around the planet and they have actually turned into an essential demand of consumers all over.

SQL or the Structured Query Language encourages the drivers to query the directories and additionally to quickly retrieve info from sources which was made already. In this particular MS SQL Server, the documents are preserved with,mdf file structure.

With SQL operating normally, information management is matchlessly simple though the genuine difficulty arises for all the owners when any trouble comes in this SQL Server.

In case you are given in place of the SQL database corruption tension that is uncalled for and fed up of the undesirable obstacle to your work due to it, then it's high time you receive an SQL Server Restoring Database application and quickly think - how you can recover SQL database effortlessly with no trouble?

Just a dependable SQL restoring repository program could be the perfect stress releaser which will take away the information loss fear and also give way to complete pleasure.

Why SQL becomes corrupted?

Sources of SQL Server corruption are really the causes needing the demand for SQL restoration. The corruption is sudden and will happen unexpectedly because of many reasons like:

Issue in hard drive

Strange and improper program shutdown accidentally

Virus and/or Trojan attack

Software or hardware malfunction

Incorrect String to multi-client collection alongside consumer deletion of Log file or collection contained "suspected" mode

No totally free disk space readily available while the working of SQL Server

While MS SQL database is operating, disk controllers attempting to access or copy the file

These are different such abrupt and unexpected explanations cause SQL crisis. It's not possible to turn the time again and avoid thing that is such to happen. Only chance with the user is thinking the way to

Restore SQL in case he with SQL 2005 and how you can restore SQL 2000 in case he's utilizing SQL Server 2000.

Mistakes appearing in the time of corruption

A person can obtain among the following mistakes in time of SQL corruption: Index' %ls' on' %ls' in database' %ls' might be corrupt due to expression evaluation changes in this particular introduction. Drop and recreate the index

The file *.mdf is lacking and must restore

Server cannot get the requested repository table

PageId in the site header = (o:o)

Table Corrupt: Object ID zero, index ID zero, page ID (1:623)

The task couldn't execute' sp_replcmds' on server internal mistake. Buffer provided reading column value is simply too little. Run DBCC CHECKDB to check out for virtually any corruption

The struggle occurred in database' table' table_name', db_name', column' column_name'. The statement was terminated

Corruption blunder of indexes, saved methods, triggers and database integrity table which must be there,MYI file is not

Know the way to restore SQL effortlessly with no difficulty?

First and primary thing which a person is necessary to do is judging whether there's a necessity for an outside SQL restoring repository application or not.

Professional assistance in the form of an SQL Server recovery device is needed if the person is acquiring one of the above mistakes cause in that situation when healing is just feasible by utilizing an external software product. SysTools SQL recovery software can fix SQL server 2005 and 2000 database files effortlessly with no difficulty.

Recovery happens easily because it takes no technical expertise and experienced software and system knowledge to perform good SQL recovery. Merely a few simple things and you are through!

Recovery happens with no difficulty because the task is sleek and there'll be no complications arising throughout the SQL repair procedure. Furthermore, the software is suitable for all of the Windows Operating system versions as Vista and ME/NT/2000/XP/2003.

CHAPTER 17

PL-SQL Instructions

PL/SQL is Oracle's Programming language or procedure language. It's so much like other programming languages. We can record particular instructions in PL/SQL which tell our applications the best way to act. PL/SQL has much equipment that significantly improve the processing of documents. PL/SQL has looping statements which allow you to do the very same run a selection of times.

Its condition logic which allows you to process records when certain circumstances are met. It's cursors that allow you to move sets of information into process and memory them one in a time. PL/SQL code is classified into structures known as blocks.

If perhaps you produce a stored package or procedure, you provide the block of PL/SQL code a title; if the block of PL/SQL code isn't given a title, then it's believed to become an anonymous block. The instances in this particular chapter will have anonymous blocks of PL/SQL code; the next chapters in this particular area illustrate the development of called blocks.

The primary distinction between PL/SQL and SQL is, In SQL's we can provide one SQl command in a period but using PL/SQL we can provide over 1 SQL command at the same time. Within a PL/SQL block, the first part will be the Declarations area. Within the Declarations section, you determine the variables and cursors which the block will wear.

The Declarations portion begins with the keyword declare and end once the Executable Commands portion starts (as suggested by "begin"). The Executable Commands portion is adhered to by the Exception Handling part; the exception keyword indicates the beginning of the Exception Handling area. The PL/SQL block is terminated by the conclusion keyword.

The framework associated with a regular PL/SQL block is displayed to the following listing: Declaration Part.

The declarative part like variable declarations, cursor declarations etc.

Execution Part.

The Executable part.

The entire programming codes are in this area.

Exception component

The exception handling area. If any mistake raised to the delivery part, the controls simply skip to the exception handling part. (Here the Declarative portion and Exception handling section are suggested. Though the Execution component is must).

Declare

The Declarative Statements.

Begin

The Statements for execution.

Exception

The Error Handling Part

End;

Declarations Section

The Declarations portion starts a PL/SQL block. The Declarations portion begins with the declare keyword, followed by a summary of adjustable and cursor definitions.

Executable Commands Section

In the Executable Commands section, you adjust the variables and cursors declared in the Declarations aisle of your PL/SQL block. The Executable Commands section usually begins with the keyword begin.

Different Handling Section

When system-related or user-defined exceptions (errors) are encountered, the command of the PL/SQL block shifts to the Exception Handling area. In the Exception Handling component, the when clause is utilized to assess what exception is to always be "raised" that is, performed.

If an exception is elevated in the Executable Commands aisle of your PL/SQL block, the flow of instructions instantly actually leaves the Executable Commands area and searches the Exception Handling aisle for an exception matching the mistake encountered. PL/SQL provides a lot of system defined exceptions and enables you to add your exceptions.

CHAPTER 18

Making Use Of An Exemplary SQL Recovery Tool To Combat SQL Data Loss

Anyone with the binary basket (the computer system) for any work type certainly handles the problem of data loss in many or the opposite thing.

This may occur because of lots of reasons which actually the person can't stay away from as bugs are a byproduct of utilizing the binary bag and till today computer programs aren't free of corruption. In each one of these scenarios, the person becomes the victim and he is the person who loses the best.

Earlier, the sole method to cope with information harm disaster was to utter a few words and after that begin the reconstruction of information from scratch once again. Seems eccentric? It certainly is!

Starting over once more right from the start and redoing the hassle each time the information is lost could certainly make some person berserk.

Thankfully, today's development is endowed with alternative methods of combating data loss issues. The best one is the usage of data recovery software tools.

Whether there's an accidental deletion of complete crash or a file of the hard disk and if the pc catches a data corrupting virus; data healing will be the answer on that the drivers may bank upon with closed eyes.

However, closing the eyes entirely during the time of picking a data recovery software program product will once again drop the person into another difficulty pit. So, choosing the best software can also be imperative.

Regrettably, the original reasons of data corruption can't be reversed or stayed away from. It's nearly impossible to keep the entry of such issues. Regardless of how vigilantly a user treads, a little virus can continue to sneak in at some or another issue, hard disks will tire out and crash frequently.

In order to cry over the spilt milk will solve no issue, but to act smarty by implementing a data recovery application will save the day for the data loss victims. Prevention is certainly a great method but while talking of computer systems, prevention might not be the sole method to deal with information loss scenarios.

The computer forensics staff will tell that entire computer system area is made on a single principle and that is - "Nothing is completely erased from computer's memory.

Each information product foliage some type or a thumbprint of remnant or trace on the system." Therefore data recovery software tools can make it possible to bargain information retrieval with data loss at virtually any corruption situation.

SQL Server Corruption

MS SQL is a good website management system to manipulate information. It's used carefully in a plethora of organizations. A corruption in SQL Server may certainly victimize some organizations and users. In such instances, every company is made to act towards getting back their crucial SQL data. If so, an SQL Recovery application will help.

CHAPTER 19

Kinds Of Advanced SQL Queries

Database programming using SQL (Structured Query Language) is crucial to construct powerful sites. Database servers are starting to be a lot more and more effective by participating in computations instead of simply passively storing information.

This implies, many of the computational jobs are now being looked after by the database servers themselves. This is possible by the use of innovative SQL query kinds. Let us discuss superior SQL query kinds.

1. SQL Queries Using' Group By' Clause

Think about that table retailers names of pupils, subjects and marks. To write a query to access the names and corresponding marks isn't hard in the least. Nevertheless, if the requirement is showing pupil names together with typical marks throughout topics, a SQL query won't be sufficient.

One of the ways is retrieving the whole data and accomplishes the necessary computations in the company layer. In case you had not identified already, internet business level will be the one wherein server code (code created using languages as PHP, J2EE, Dot Net) resides. Nevertheless, in case you understand writing queries having' Group By' clause, you might perfectly complete calculations in the database level itself.

2. SQL Triggers

Queries tend to be invoked by server programming languages as PHP,J2EE etc. Nevertheless, there might be instances when one needs to invoke a certain query based on the output associated with a prior query. These are kinds of automatic jobs using SQL Triggers are available in extremely concurrent (busy) uses.

3. SQL Stored Procedures

To optimize the amount of lines of code is crucial in order to enhance efficiency and also to lower throughput period. Among the factors that influence the amount of lines of code will be the dimensions of SQL queries.

Saved Procedures may considerably decrease the quantity of lines of code needed by SQL queries. They are modular functions which can be called from anyplace with specified parameters. With saved procedures, the code gets reusable and modular.

4. SQL Aggregate Functions

Aggregate features assistance programmers to do businesses on an array of details in a column. They may operate simultaneously on many rows. A good example for aggregate functionality is' average( )'. This particular feature, when used on many columns, the end result will be a computed typical of all of the values.

In the lack of a function, the company layer coder has to calculate typical using following steps.

1) Firstly, the coder must count the amount of columns being operated on

2) Secondly, the coder must strip away null values coming from the selected columns.

3) Finally he is to compute typical utilizing mathematical formulas.

CHAPTER 20

The Best Way To Fix A Corrupt SQL Database (Multiple IAM Pages Error 8947)

Worldwide Allocation Page (GAM) of SQL Server File: An MS SQL Server file is composed of different pages, that place its allocation structures. One particular web page will be the Global Allocation Page (GAM). It has the info that is connected to the allotted extents within that SQL Server file.

Index Allocation Map (IAM) Pages: An Index Allocation Map (IAM) page is the allocation web pages that have info of the extents which an index/table uses.

SQL Table Corruption Because of Multiple IAM Pages Error: Sometimes, you many encounter errors because of multiple IAM web pages for one item. This kind of mistakes indicates table corruption. The error you may encounter after that corruption inside your SQL Server repository table states:

Server: Msg 8947, Level sixteen, State one Table error:

Multiple IAM web pages for object index ID I_ID ID O_ID, have allocations for the identical interval. And IAM pages P_ID1 and P_ID2.

Exactly why Such Error Might Occur?

In case you are encountering the above mentioned mistake, subsequently it means the IAM chain for the specified index has no less than two IAM pages (P_ID1 and P_ID) addressing the identical GAM interval (interval will be the file area utilized by the GAM page to chart. It's around four GB).

Every list, and that is issued from the GAM interval which has greater than 1 degree, demands the IAM page for that soecific GAM interval.

For those GAM interval, the IAM page has a single bit for every degree. The set bit shows the specific index is awarded to such index. A typical reason behind the multiple IAM pages error you could be encountering could be hardware failure. SQL database recovery becomes needed for you in this instance.

How you can Fix Damaged MDF File? You can perform the next techniques for SQL database recovery:

• Replace Damaged Hardware: First of all, you have to check out if there's some problem associated with hardware failure. Because of this, you can function hardware diagnostics and check the application, Windows and SQL Server error log. When such problem exists, replace the impaired hardware (when required).

• SQL Database Recovery from Backup: If you have a thoroughly clean backup for the SQL database, next you can effortlessly regain from it. Nevertheless, if no such legitimate backup is there, next you can use a third party tool.

SQL Database Recovery utilizing Third party Tool: You can purchase an SQL MDF repair application, which is a simple, effective, time-saving and safe method to address the issue.

One such strong SQL repository recovery device is SysTools SQL Recovery application. It's an excellent tool with a user friendly interface and it employs technology that is advanced for efficient recovery and quick algorithms for brief MDF repair.

This particular application can effectively respond to your questions such as - "How to examine corrupt MDF?" and the way to fix corrupt SQL data?" Overall, SysTools SQL Recovery program could maybe be the best apt option you could get for SQL repository restoration.

CHAPTER 21

SQL Database Recovery Post Table Corruption

SQL database table is a team of specific number of columns and rows that have huge records chunks. DBA can get the necessary data pertaining to his needs from the table, by managing a query.

The database query and in many instances displays attractive outcomes, may fail because of different factors. One of the more common aspects for failure is corruption of table.

Not many recognized aspects for table corruption are incorrect method shutdown, virus attack,, application failure and metadata structure corruption. In the majority of cases of query execution disaster, an error message becomes shown on the computer monitor.

This particular error message includes all required info that can help a DBA to determine the amount of corruption and the best way to conquer it. Nevertheless, if a DBA is not able to recognize the error message and does not have any backup of database, then simply SQL database recovery becomes a bit of tough.

To clarify the above mentioned error message, here is a real time scenario. A person would like to count the amount of rows of table that he executes count(*) query. Nevertheless, the query rather than exhibiting the entire number displays the under error message:

"Attempt to fetch rational page (1:42724) in database' test' belongs to object' report-table', not to object' RRR'. Connection Broken.."

Knowing the dinner table is corrupted, the person tries DBCC Checktable command with repair_rebuild parameter to learn the amount of corruption. The command displays the under result:

"Server: Msg 2535, Level sixteen, State one, Line one Table Corrupt: Page (1:42724) is issued to object ID 1517248460, index ID zero, not to object ID 982294559, index ID zero discovered with site header.

Server: Msg 8939, Level sixteen, State one, Line one Table Corrupt: Object ID 1517248460, index ID zero, web page (1:42723). Test (m_freeCnt == freeCnt) failed. Values are 1468 and 8066.

The database table files are inaccessible post the above mentioned error message appears. The individual additionally attempts DBCC CHECKDB command with repair_allow_data_loss parameter. But nothing works.

Resolution:

In these kinds of cases, the safest and best method is repairing the database table is by utilizing SQL Recovery application.

MS SQL Recovery Software Information:

A SQL recovery program may be used by anybody. The database table files remain secure and could be viewed before restoration. This kind of SQL repository recovery items include a free trial version that can be downloaded and also placed on all Windows os's.

CHAPTER 22

SQL Server Virtualization

SQL Server virtualization is starting to be more prevalent, but it is not always simple to buy it perfect. Think about the following SQL Server virtualization suggestions before you start.

1. Plan, plan, and also arrange a few much more. Much like nearly all complicated tasks, your ultimate success begins long time before you can get your hands on the task itself. Consider what you would like to achieve and discover just what it will take to help you there.

Pick an effort breakdown framework to break everything into simple tasks. Look at everything such as your available resources, existing infrastructure, and new technologies. When we do this first Planning on paper, you can count on difficulties - and resolve them - before they happen.

2. Learn about the most prevalent pitfalls you are more likely to encounter when applying SQL Server virtualization. For instance, storage problems including misconfigured disk consolidation, performance, and disks usually catch administrators off guard.

By studying these pitfalls before you start, you can get ready for them. Various other typical pitfalls include: using the incorrect hypervisor style, mismanaging memory, misunderstanding performance benchmarks, and incorrect disk partitioning.

3. Watch pertinent SQL Server virtualization video clips. While you can go to classes or sign up for an internet program, you might be able to find useful movies on the internet which prepare you for all the challenges ahead.

4. Use the appropriate processor on the virtualization host. Ideally, the virtualization host must have a 64 bit, SLAT enabled processor. Do not take SLAT (Second Level Address Translation) as a given as not all 64 bit processors, particularly older ones, support it. SLAT provides for improved virtual machine efficiency and scalability.

5. If you have SQL Server 2008 Enterprise Edition (or higher) together with virtual devices which support "hot add RAM," consider utilizing powerful memory. Powerful mind enables buffers to increase or contract to accommodate altering workloads.

6. Go for a one-to-one ratio between your virtual cores and CPUs. This ensures adequate processing power at all of times for the challenges of SQL Server.

7. Use the suitable virtual hard disk process for your needs. For instance, in case your server runs manufacturing workloads, choose a fixed virtual hard disk instead of a dynamic body.

Fixed virtual hard disks demand much more disk space than dynamic shoes but offer a greater level of performance.

When efficiency is not important, but room restrictions are, then a dynamic virtual hard disk will be a more sensible choice. Similarly, in case you want the greatest performance possible, a pass through disk might worth your consideration.

8. Customize the virtual server instance. Although easy to recognize, the default feature is not often the most desirable option. For instance, in case your workloads demand top performance storage, recognizing the default virtual hard disk would probably result in disappointing overall performance.

You might want to assign virtual hard disks or different pass-through disks for your log files, operating system, and data. Be sure you understand the different disk implementation options and select probably the very best configuration for your unique needs that may or might not be the default option.

Preparation, learning about everyday pitfalls, and selecting the proper configuration choices for your needs are crucial components to an excellent SQL Server virtualization task.

CHAPTER 23

SQL Server Security Updates

Microsoft has a complete new approach towards the security. In their own words: "We will rethink our approach to security. We will examine our code for vulnerabilities. We will release patches as necessary.

We will turn off most characteristics by default to keep the footprint modest. In case you want a thing, switch it on. But in case you do not need it, leave it all. The means in case vulnerability is found in an item you are not using, you will not be affected."

The newest SQL Servers has come up with a lot of extra protection features; these functions not just create the database much more safe, but additionally much more explicable and much easier to handle.

Database programs could be created by the programmers, whilst operating and the exact privileges needed, with the additional new capabilities. This particular element is known as "the concept of minimum privilege." A coder isn't an additional forced to operate like a SA (System Administrator) or DBA (Database Administrator).

Many of the key new features which have been added to the newest model of the server, are as follows:

Security for.NET

A mix of various SQL Server permissions,.NET code security and Windows permissions have to administer and execute the.NET code. Three unique amounts are used-to resolve regarding just what a code can't or could do outdoors and inside of SQL Server.

The Password policies for all the owners of SQL Server If running the SQL Server on a Win 2003 Server, then the consumers can go by the related policies as for integrated security users.

In order to Map a SQL Server user to Windows credentials

The owners of SQL Server can use Windows credentials once they get access to the outside energy for example community shares and documents.

Separating schemas and owners Schemas in a SQL Server mention the 1st category items which may be run by a person, group, a role or application roles. The simple fact that the meaning of synonyms is permitted, make it really much easier to administer.

Permissions grant

It's not necessary for users or logins to have many specific roles being particular permissions; many are grantable with REVOKE, GRANT and Deny verbs.

Refreshing protection on the Server's metadata

One isn't permitted to immediately upgrade the new metadata views, moreover just if a person has permissions to particular metadata regarding certain items, he can list them.

Assistance of encryption keys and certificates

The newest security functions enable the server to control encryption keys and certificates, because using with Web Services SSL, with Service Broker, for fresh data encryption, and also with code authentication.

Above are but many of the countless new security features the SQL is with.

Though it will assist you to in providing a little thought about the way the Microsoft has attempted to work tirelessly in fixing some security loopholes in the existing variations of the SQL Server, and also the way they have created it a lot safer compared to the past types of this particular server.

CHAPTER 24

SQL Server: Advanced Protection

To protect your SQL databases can suggest saving thousands for your company in conditions of ensuring efficiency, meeting regulation specifications, and also preventing downtime and data loss. Allow me to share a handful of tricks and tips to make certain that your SQL databases are deployed properly and available if the information is needed most.

Besides the information itself, a SQL server contains the transaction log and the method databases. Both should be thoroughly protected whether the application is going to be smoothly restored.

See your Workloads around Backup Windows

SQL backups could be carried out while consumers are definitely querying the database and transactions will be processed. SQL backups utilize a lot of system resources, particularly I/O, therefore it is better to do intensive, full backups if the device is experiencing mild load times.

Shorten Data Backups

When general efficiency is suffering because of long backup windows, many measures could be brought to lessen the time that the method is doing a backup. One method to reduce should be to backup to disk.

When you are backing up to disk before offloading to some other backup process, be careful to not backup to the identical disk which is utilized to keep the database and transaction.

To copy the database to its own array can avoid I/O overload and also guarantee the database can be purchased in the event associated with a main system failure.

Utilize Different Backup Methods

SQL server provides various backup methods full, differential, and transaction backups. Right now there are included in the SQL server. Picking out the back-up method depends mostly on your environment. Specifically, it is determined by what size the database it's and how crucial the database is usually to your business.

Full backups can weigh down your servers and storage systems, therefore plan carefully how frequently you need to perform a complete backup versus transactional or differential backups.

Little databases that aren't far too big and change infrequently may be backed up only every day or weekly. Transactional databases which are mission critical must be backup up as frequently as you can.

Backup Transaction Logs Frequently

Then to the database, transaction logs are the most crucial details in a SQL server database. The log discusses activity and also may be utilized to conduct PiT (point-in-time) restorations.

Remember: the transactional backup just backs as much as the final transactional backup, so a complete restore might suggest doing many transactional backups to be able to completely resort the database.

The transactional log must be performed every 10 minutes for very active databases, and at the very least many times one day.

Backing Up SQL System Databases

The device databases will be the other essential part of a SQL server program, such as both master and msdb. But there contain essential data including system configuration and are needed in the event of an entire restore. Nevertheless, the device databases alter less often and must be backed up a minimum of weekly, or every day in case it's an especially active database.

Among the biggest elements which has an effect on protection and performance of the Microsoft SQL server is the I/O of the disk subsystem.

Backups and Storage Growth

Multiple backups can develop considerable storage fees as total, differential, and transactional backups are carried out for effective SQL systems on a routine schedule. Below are a few ways to control expenses, and guarantee the information is adequately backed up.

Offload backups to its own, low-cost storage array. This particular training guarantees high performance, high cost disk is freed in place for established databases.

Planning for growth up front can prevent pricey, final minute's storage purchases. When buying storage space array from Reliant Technology, your storage consultant will help you adequately forecast your database growth and make sure you have plenty inexpensive, high capacity disk to effectively protect program and transactional logs for your databases.

Constantly Place Log Files on RAID 1+0 (or RAID one) Disks Placing databases and log files on RAID ten could significantly enhance performance and also offer good protection from hardware failure.

With much better write performance, your system will avoid errors and corruption.

Note: Generally RAID 1+0 will offer better throughput for write intensive applications. The quantity of efficiency received will be different based upon the HW vendor's RAID implementations. Many common substitute for RAID 1+0 is RAID five.

In general, RAID 1+0 provides much better create performance compared to every other RAID level providing information protection, like RAID five.

CHAPTER 25

Issues To Think About Whenever Choosing SQL Database Backup Services

Whatever sort of SQL database you are operating, in case you do not get an SQL backup in position and operating all of the time, disaster is merely a couple of steps away. It's just about sure that the SQL will fail at a while of the future, and if it's due to user error, an all-natural disaster, or a virus - you'll spend the cost in case your SQL backup program isn't operating.

Small companies are known for not taking proper care of their data, and also it comes as an extensive shock to them whenever they enter their office one day, and then discover they are of business.

When your entire billing system, employee database, and client information is resting on an SQL server, in case you do not get an SQL backup in position, you'll essentially have stolen anything you have, and you will find very few businesses which can conquer that sort of damage.

If you go looking for a backup program, you will find two basics that you need to ensure you have. To begin with, it's to be simple enough for you (or another person in your company) to make use of it. It should not need the expertise of a specialist or the company's Mensa fellow member to load it up and get hold of it running.

Secondly, you ought to be in a position to recover your data in a situation of minutes with no hassle. There are many applications which enable you making incremental backups, so that in case your backup is corrupted, there'll nonetheless be many unblemished information generally there that you can pull from.

You should additionally be searching for a system that can run by itself, based on a routine that you set. By doing this, you won't ever need to be worried about your backup once again, realizing that it will be there if you want it.

In case you are likely to appear for SQL database backup products on the web, your search would most likely go back million, outcomes. The large number of service providers by itself signifies that there's great distinction in between the amounts of service they provide.

Hence, the person is often confused regarding which provider to decide to provide assistance regarding how to backup SQL database. To help you on this task, you will need to think about a few things to be able to arrive at a convenient ultimate decision.

The first thing you have to think about is whether you can maintain your copy of your data while with a database backup. Having your copy of your files will enable you to bring them at the very best speed.

Without your data, your chosen provider will have to transmit them over the process and the net will take an extended time to complete. If perhaps you have a small company with a 1.5 mbps downloading velocity, for instance, it will take around 14 hours to transmit information comprising of 10 gigabytes.

Your chosen SQL repository backup provider will typically encrypt your data while it's in transit and when it gets to the information center. Many of the readily available providers giving SQL restore solutions are just encrypting info throughout the transmission.

You have to additionally have the ability to watch the amount of protection used by the database restore provider and also the type of information facility that it's. Generally there ought to be unwanted power, generator and Internet run moment to safeguard against power loss. Extra things you must take into account are background clearances, authentication, firewalls, and physical security.

In case your selected SQL database backup service provider doesn't use newspapers to run its office, it should have a consistent information protection or CDP. This ought to be worn by the provider to back up its data since there aren't any paper trails to replicate documents if there's a data loss.

It must be operated by experts who actually understand how to backup SQL and should have a support for all of the database platforms it uses, like Oracle and MSSQL. In order to boost flexibility and support, some SQL database backup websites will let you provide a pre and post command to databases. Generally, the science utilized additionally lets backup multi treaded scheduling.

In case you are lucky adequate to have programming abilities, it's doable to create an SQL server backup software that can automate the backing up of information. But for more complicated tasks, you will have to employ SQL database backup software program.

This is better in the end since writing your script and debugging it will take effort and time more than buying a solution which has been prepared and effectively planned by professionals in the company. You'll additionally have the possibility of picking probably the most ideal for your business, since you will find plenty of firms competing in the marketplace.

Chapter 26

SQL Data Recovery

Despite having the intrinsic information protection readily available in an SQL server repository process the necessity of SQL information healing can't be totally stayed away from.

Despite the availability of various other data protection measures like hard disk crashes, redundant array of disks, and other inadvertent problems can lead to corruption of the perfect information file and the backup file of an SQL database.

During these kinds of events, the function of a database administrator gets a lot more crucial. He should make sure that the database should be up and running once again as soon as they can.

The database administrator of a business understands the occurrence of a database crash with partial information loss can't be accepted by the business. This is especially when that data especially affects the business bottom line and its relation with its customers.

Many data source administrators are conscious of the havoc which partial corruption of the perfect information file of a database can result in.

The database management system (DBMS) has plenty of safeguards as backup techniques to safeguard the company's vital information kept in the website. Nevertheless, it still is feasible that actually the transaction logs and also the backups become corrupted.

Thus, smart database administrators constantly think about the job of professional SQL data recovery application. They currently have in position the application that can help recover practically all information from corrupted, ,bak documents and mdf files of the database.

This kind of application can be purchased on the market in the kind of customizable package or an on-the-shelf from information healing consulting businesses. It's additionally offered from many companies in the type of a program as a service.

The second form is hosted on a site of the company which develops it. The Web based software is particularly helpful for businesses with massive work and databases in the distributed atmosphere.

With all the usage of such particular program it's feasible to recover information from the following.

It can help recover information from damaged RAID hard drives, removed or corrupted indexes, deleted and damaged tables, table information or partly corrupted schema.

It can assist in recovery from deleted or damaged foreign or primary keys or a locked.mdf or database (master information file) file. It can assist do this from deleted stored methods or missing triggers. It can additionally assist recover information from misplaced and fallen tables, accidental deletion of volumes or tables.

Additionally, the application can help recovering lost information from just about all types of SQL server. The standard information healing time taken for data recovery is generally from one to four times.

This is determined by the seriousness of the information corruption and the root cause of the database crash. The SQL data recovery software application thus can serve as a good bulwark against the likelihood of power failures, database crashes and inadvertent operations.

CHAPTER 27

Software Testing With SQL Table Audit

Just about the most crucial areas in SQATesters qualities of a great tester is being suspicious, but exactly how does this apply to program testing? It means not trusting exactly what the software tells you but choosing other evidence to confirm that your test was a success.

The concept of utilizing an auditing application for tests is easy,

The auditing application will record each information shift on the website or a certain set of tables, next you can utilize the information in the audit log to confirm that your tests are a success.

So what's SQL Table Audit?

It's a tool which installs table triggers to your database to record all data switches for audited tables. It's extensive audit log filtering and viewing capabilities for finding out just the way the information is changing in your database.

A basic example; Imagine you are testing a set of CRUD operations for saved addresses. You upgrade a current tackle then check that the tackles have been updated by utilizing the address perspective page/form inside the application.

The modification seems to have worked, great... or could it be. Might it be what has occurred will be the software has updated its cached version of the information although not really persisted many changes on the website. A simple method of learning is checking the review log for the website.

Finding the information changes that your tests have caused is simple. SQL Table Audit has effective audit air filtering abilities which enable you to locate modifications by table, time and date, kind (insert, update, delete), the information which changed (old worth and new worth), columns, application and user.

An excellent job flow for testers applying SQL Table Audit is to; Add auditing to the entire database or selected tables, Perform the test, now examine the audit log to make sure that the appropriate information obtained current, placed or deleted.

Testing could mean repeating the identical test using various parameters. By utilizing the effective rewind functionality provided you can rewind information changes that have occurred in the course of an exam, now try the test once again. This could save hours of labor resetting or redeploying a test environment.

After tests, SQL Table Audit can clean up when itself by eliminating all auditing items through the database.

By utilizing business standard equipment as SQL Table Audit by you can help reduce the danger of bugs being shipped and enhance the quality of application you try.

CHAPTER 28

SQL Database Backup - Things You Have To Know

Regardless of what business type you are operating, learning how to backup SQL database would regularly be crucial to be able to safeguard important information which you have to put your business. SQL database backup can be achieved by way of a remote file server for improved business security.

You can often backup your data locally with the usage of a USB, CD/DVD or in your local hard drive, which has got the benefit of enabling you to access the information which you like fast and easily. However, you never ever know what can occur. In case a disaster strikes, like a flood or fire, you might lose your data indefinitely.

An SQL database backup over a remote server has a number of benefits with a local one. Your data are kept in a protected place outside of your house or business location, that will provide you with much more peace of mind. Whatever happens with your personal computer or to your workplace, your important data would always remain there.

The majority of the huge, multinational corporations make use of this method in safeguarding their essential business information.

The ones that are on outsourcing additionally profit a lot out of a remote SQL restore program simply because the information from multinational companies are secure in their countries while simultaneously being employed by their foreign sites. This will give them an assurance that their data are secure.

In case you are searching for a collection restore service provider, you will find many features that you will have to check. For starters, obviously, is constant protection for your data.

There's a lot of software to select from available, though you have to have one which will capture and track changes constantly with no input from you. Your selected collection backup remote server should also enjoy a function that every backup service provider needs to have, and this is information reduplication.

What this means is that a selection of back up applications exist that provides back up for many copies of the same information. The task just saves documents which were transformed rather than having a backup for all things. This fact by itself will enable you to save ninety 9 % of your bandwidth and time.

If perhaps you recognize the way to back up SQL, subsequently it's feasible to create SQL server backup software of one's own. But this kind of a plan can entail a large amount of time in perfecting, and the reality that you are attending to other things in the identical time.

If you can avail of a program from the Internet whose only focus may be the safety of your precious data, then why burden yourself unnecessarily. There's a registration procedure you will need to complete the

moment you have settled upon an internet SQL repository backup provider, but the moment it's finished, the task is straightforward and simple pretty.

A program specific to your needs will need to be downloaded to your personal computer, which is user-friendly, even by someone with little understanding of computers and software.

At this point, the majority of individuals understand the web is heavy with viruses and that regardless of how healthy you train your employees; the viruses will really make their way in your computer system.

When you are operating a SQL server and also have many customers, the importance of owning an SQL backup is huge since you simply don't know if the next virus will hit. All kinds, adware, spamware, and viruses of uses are out there, simply waiting to eliminate your data.

Naturally, a virus is just one reason creating an SQL backup is very critical. One more reason is the fact that accidents happen. No matter whether it's an all-natural disaster, like a fire or a flood, or a power surge which fries your server, you'll appreciate having a message of your data prepared for use.

Perhaps even in case you reside or operate in a location which isn't subject to flooding, earthquakes, or hurricanes, you simply don't know when a pipe will spring a leak, if the sprinklers go off of, and when someone will drop a cup of espresso directly into the server.

Lastly, the final reason, and maybe the most typical reason behind developing an SQL backup prepared to go is simply because there are usually individuals on the market who would not mind performing you or your company a bit of damage.

Whether these are competitors, ex-employees, or current employees with a grudge, it's not at all unusual for individuals to intentionally delete information, ruin a server, or let viruses loose in a product.

With a backup, you will allow yourself a lot much more flexibility to do the job, realizing that should anything happen, you'll have the ability to easily retrieve. Creating an SQL server backup is similar to have an insurance policy for your data, and it's one which the majority of businesses can't afford to be without nowadays.

SQL backup is a fantastic tool which can backup the data or any other essential files. Its other uses also and also can develop much more databases in addition to tables which are within the database. Additionally, it updates the database and will complete will, deletions, and insertions develop procedures.

For people who are not truly into creating all of your files once more, this could be the best tool and program to have. Personal computer crashes aren't any fun, so the reason add to the aggravation and aggravation of being forced to replicate it all again?

While a number of individuals could have extra backups someplace, it is generally a great item to possess much more as this can definitely guarantee each little bit of info you have is readily accessible in the regrettable event of any crash.

Consider all of the valuable things you have on your computer. This may be something from financial records for your business to private photo memories.

An SQL backup application can in many cases offer more when compared to a typical backup program can. Things are kept healthy. Additionally, it has the additional feature to allow for other applications. This restores each database you have and can make use of over one thread to do it.

While some may think it is a bad idea to have, this specific backup plan is helpful. What occurs if your other backup gets lost and damaged? You are left with nothing, while this program can stop that from occurring. Getting back on the internet is crucial and is designed for the most part good for you too.

Make An SQL Backup You can Rely On

At this point, most companies have some kind of backup for their data. The normal issue is it's also presently not running, or no one knows the way to restore the information after a crash. If perhaps you have a SQL server and do not possess a separate SQL backup running, you can actually end up going out of business immediately.

The fact is that installing and managing a SQL backup is very simple in case you select the best product and also have some fundamental networking knowledge. And then, setting it to jog is similar to establishing an alarm clock, and also you should not have to perform something different.

The main distinction between many different SQL backup programs is where and how the backups are produced. As for how they are created, you can often have a backup that is performed in whole, at particular intervals. You can additionally select partial or incremental backups which will allow you going further back in time, in the event your backup is as corrupted as your live data is.

The location of your backup is probably the most crucial facet that you need to be thinking about. You definitely cannot have your backup relaxing in the same building as your data. The reasons for this are apparent, though many organizations fail to recognize just how crucial it is.

Consider in case your building is flooded, burns on the floor, and is swept away in a tornado. If perhaps your backup is within the exact same structure, it will do you no good at all.

Thus, be sure you have an excellent backup, one is up-to-date and checked frequently, and also make sure that it's located somewhere apart from the place you keep your data. This helps to make sure that you usually have a backup going to when the much worse really does take place and your company.

CHAPTER 29

Database Snapshots in SQL Server

Actually wanted to create a read-only point-in-time message of a data source, and wondered which method to use?

Microsoft SQL Server 2005 offers a plethora of methods to accomplish this, such as database backup/restore, mirroring, replication, log-shipping, and database detaches/re M attaches, so forth. Nevertheless, one strategy readily available in the Enterprise edition, the Database Snapshot, is new to SQL Server 2005, and it is well worth taking a better look.

Precisely why are Database Snapshots Useful?

There are lots of applications in which a point-in-time snapshot is helpful. Microsoft suggests the next utilize cases:

Reporting up to a particular period of time, ignoring later data

Reporting against standby or mirror databases which are usually unavailable

Insuring against consumer or administrator error, giving a fast way to return to an older model of the database

Managing test databases, especially during quick element and schema growth Of course, these requirements might be helped by a database backup or connected text of a data source, though the primary key advantage of picking a picture more than among another techniques is simple: creating a database snapshot is rapidly.

Using and creating Database Snapshots Creating database snapshots is not hard - it is a make Database statement, specifying just the physical and logical filenames. Remember it is a read only snapshot, therefore we do not have to add transaction log settings or autogrowth. Here is the code:

Create Database AdventureWorks_Snapshot_Monday ON

FILENAME='C:SnapshotsAD2K_Monday.ss')

(NAME=AdventureWorks_Data,

AS Snapshot OF AdventureWorks

Snapshot development isn't backed by Object Explorer user interface in the Management Studio; you need to make use of a make Database statement, along with the AS Snapshot OF clause showing the supply website. Additionally, remember that just the Enterprise edition of SQL Server 2005 supports repository pictures.

The snapshot has a version of the information as it existed at creation, rolled again uncommitted transactions. Which means that usually unavailable databases, like mirrors and standby servers, may be utilized to produce pictures?

To have developed a picture, you can today put it to use as you had other read only database; most items are uncovered in precisely the exact same manner, through Object Explorer, scripts, and reporting equipment.

Reverting a database on the edition kept in the picture is similarly easy:

DATABASE_SNAPSHOT='AdventureWorks_Snapshot_Monday'

Restore Database AdventureWorks FROM

It returns the database to the state it had been in once the snapshot is developed, minus some uncommitted transactions - keep in mind that a snapshot is constant at its creation. Remember that snapshot restoration produces any other snapshots useless - they ought to be deleted and re-created when needed.

How can Database Snapshots function?

A Database Snapshot is like a regular read only database, out of the user's point of view; it could be seen with a Use statement, and may be browsed from inside Management Studio.

Nevertheless, it originally occupies very little disk space, therefore may be produced very quickly. This particular magic is achieved through sparse files and an NTFS feature. A sparse file is such a file which might seem to be big, but actually just consumes a percentage of the actual physical space allocated to it.

Today, as a database snapshot presents a read only view of the source database, it will need not keep a copy of every web page.

Rather, SQL Server performs a copy-on-write operation; in the resource database, the first time a data page changes after the construction of a picture, a copy of the initial web page is positioned in the sparse file. Also the snapshot serves details from the snapshot copies wherein supply information has changed, and the initial source pages when they are unchanged.

Optimum Practices

Often you will choose a copy of a backup more than a picture, at times it will be a detached message of the information file. Nevertheless, for lots of cases your best bet is a database picture, therefore it is really worth keeping many points in mind. In particular:

The file size will look substantially bigger compared to the area it consumes on disk, and must be definitely marked as a snapshot because of this. Pick explicit naming events making it obvious to administrators.

Snapshots are at their greatest when fresh and young, and do not occupy a lot of room. Should you have to keep a snapshot for just about any period of time, think about using another method to create the read-only copies.

As snapshots persist till it isdeleted, you will need to rotate snapshots, either by hand or with a software.

Also, performing index operations including defragmentation or index rebuilding will modify a lot of pages that the snapshot will probably contain a total copy of the cause details for that index. The greater number of snapshots you will find, the greater number of copies will exist.

Whenever the disk containing a picture fills up, and a web page create fails, the snapshot becomes ineffective, as it won't include all needed pages. Make sure the disk cannot fill up!

Database snapshots are a valuable inclusion to the arsenal of every SQL Server DBA, and also fit in perfectly and other methods, especially when you might have to rapidly revert a database, or in case you have to keep rolling pictures.

Consider the primary key advantages: excessive speed and minimal actual physical size. But additionally keep in mind that these benefits diminish when the snapshot ages and expands, of course, if the quantity of snapshots increases.

Above most, database snapshots are quick and very easy to use; it will not set you back something to test them out, and also you'll likely discover them really helpful indeed. In case all that you have to do with a point-in-time message is select from it, or return to it, subsequently a database snapshot is very likely the greatest option offered.

CHAPTER 30

SQL Server Performance

When views had been initially explained to me, they had been discussed improperly. I have, since that time, heard others regurgitate exactly the same falsehood countless occasions.

I operated under this phony awareness for a long time until recently, dealing with Query Analyzer and also breaking down the query plans, I watched "the light."

Many of us had been taught that Views are more slowly since the database must calculate them before they are employed to join to various other tables and prior to the way in which clauses are utilized.

When you have plenty of tables at the view, then this method ultimately slows everything down. This explanation appears to be realistic on the counter, and it is therefore readily accepted. Nevertheless, there is nothing further from the reality on SQL Server!

The simple fact of the issue is the fact that whenever a query is now being digested by the SQL Server's optimizer, it examines the areas inside the select to discover which seem to be required by the consuming query.

When it requires a certain area, subsequently it extracts it from the query definition, together with its table from the From clause, and any restrictions it requires out of the Where clause or additional clauses (GROUP BY, Having, etc.)

These extracted elements are next merged into the eating queries and are usually treated as being a sub query. The optimizer subsequently joins the information together along indexes as best it can, just like it can with non-view components, after which the whole query is run. The view isn't pre calculated simply because the query chunk came out of a view definition.

Thus, so why views usually run slower than exactly the same code do typed straight into a query? 3 reasons:

Reason one - Sort Order: Sub queries frequently are afflicted by not remaining sequenced in an order which could effortlessly be merged into the key query. This leads to the server to do additional work to and so the information returned by the sub query before merging it. In this particular circumstance, the information is pre calculated so it could be sorted.

Reason two - Inner Joins: If the point of view is divided to discover what fields on the select are required, after which the corresponding table from the clause, it's going one step further. It should think about something in the where clause which could throw out data.

Too, Inner Joins from the dinner table inthe from clause may also throw out information if the joined in table doesn't possess a coordinating row. Since the optimizer does not know if the Inner Join was utilized as a filtering printer, it's to add in it.

Often, tables are joined in showing details which the consuming query does not require, not only as a filter. In these instances, the Inner Join just causes SQL Server to perform far more work for no valid reason.

Side note: Left Joins aren't utilized as air filters. In case a View remaining joins in a table, but there aren't any fields utilized in that table, it'll be removed once the point of view is pulled to.

Explanation three - Redundant Tables Calls: Whenever you produce a point of view, you can really make use of an additional perspective as a supply of information.

This practice could be nested virtually limitlessly. Since each one of these ideas will likely be have the query definitions pulled in as a Sub Query, then it is extremely likely that exactly the same base table will take part in the query many times. This is, generally, only a waste. Precisely why go to the identical place many times?

CHAPTER 31

SQL Server Indexes

Many of us understand that indexes can help our software queries to perform faster but few people understand whether the database motor will in fact use those indexes or not. So I am hoping that by the conclusion of this chapter you will be ready to identify when you should create indexes and maximize your use of them.

What exactly are SQL Server indexes?

SQL Server applies indexes the same as you make use of the guide index to retrieve a topic. Say you have to find out about subject X in a publication, you'll merely go the list and hunt for the quantity of pages where X is brought up. SQL Server does the identical thing; it uses the list as being a guide to access information from a particular family table.

Clustered indexes: Among the best illustrations to show just how does a clustered index work is the fact that of a telephone book. Each telephone book entry belongs to a row in a kitchen table.

Our index here must be based upon the last and first name, thus in case you are searching for somebody who is last name is "Smith" you will looking for pages having family names starting with "S".

Once you reach the appropriate web page, you'll make use of the first brand to reach the appropriate entry. This procedure is really called "Index Seek".

Today let's suppose you would like to get all persons having a first name "Mark". This is achievable, but since your phone book is sorted by last name then and first by name that is first, therefore you'll be made to proceed through all entries in the telephone book for getting the preferred outcome. This is named "Index Scan", an exhausting operation on great tables.

The mechanism associated with a clustered index is pretty easy. The thought is sorting the information in the table based on the information in the list column (using a B Tree structure) therefore SQL Server can fetch the specific row(s) faster.

A B Tree is a data structure which supports quickly searching with a minimum amount of disk reads, and this is what allows our data source motor to promptly get the query effect.

Remember that you can have one and just one clustered index on any table, because the information can be sorted in a single order physically.

Non-Clustered indexes:

A non-clustered index has the indexed column additionally to a sharp to the particular row of information. A online search engine is an excellent example, each time you research on Google, the end result you receive is a pair of link to existing websites, therefore you have to click all of these website link to get "more" info.

The exact same is true for SQL Server, if the info you need to have are integrated to the list, then you are finished, or else you have to head to the particular rows of information.

We watched the benefits that indexes provide, but how about the disadvantages?

Disk space Indexes occupy an amount of disk space when they are developed which amount keeps on increasing as your data expands. This may be a disadvantage in case you are restricted on disk space.

Data manipulation When you do a modification your table data, whether it is Insert, Update or DELETE, your database engine will need to update all complex indexes, and this is a pricey operation. Hence you ought to take into account just how regular does your data get modified when you are intending to develop an index on every table.

CHAPTER 32

The Secrets To Choosing An SQL Backup

As somebody who's in control of an SQL server, you have an enormous task on your hands. You have to be sure that the server is running and the information isn't corrupt.

You have to ensure all employees' info is secure and that they have uninterrupted access to their data. Lastly, you additionally have to ensure that will something happen to possibly the server or among the users' pcs, that there's an SQL backup running.

To this day, you will find a lot of firms that are not backing up their SQL servers. This is completely absurd since the chance of your information becoming corrupted is really quite high. Nearly all individuals believe in terminology of their server getting destroyed in some sort of a catastrophe, but you'll find some other things which is possible also.

When you are selecting an SQL backup application, probably the most crucial thing to bear in mind is ease of use. When it's way too hard to use, or demands some sort of specialized knowledge, you won't ever put it to use.

And, in case you do not put it to use, you will not have a backup. Simply creating an SQL backup offer sitting on the shelf will not enable you to one bit when your server goes down.

You must additionally pick a plan which enables you to back up the information to an offsite source and up into "the cloud". In that way, you will be certain to get a secure copy of your data in case your building is destroyed or in case your server is irrecoverable.

This might look farfetched, though you would not function as the 1st business that was destroyed by a server which had become corrupted and afflicted by a lot of viruses which it simply could not be rebooted, so get backed up now.

A large amount of individuals who are highly trained in info technology neglect to recognize the benefits of having a dependable backup for their SQL server.

Because this application type is currently so affordable and extremely simple to use, it is astonishing that more people are not running it on a routine basis. It appears that it usually is not until you drop all of your data which you understand a SQL backup application may have saved you.

You'll find a couple of things you need to look for in case you are considering purchasing a SQL backup application, the first of which will be the simplicity of use. An application that is not simple to use won't get installed, not to mention run correctly.

This is usually the situation with the more complex backup programs. Somebody buys it, though nobody understands the way to run it, therefore it rests on the shelf and it is no good in the least.

An SQL backup application mustn't merely be simple to use, though it ought to be simple to bring the information from. Put simply, having the ability to back up with ease is but one factor, though you need

to additionally be easily and quickly capable to bring your data. Having a backup that you simply cannot work from isn't a good to anyone, as ensure that whatever package you purchase is simple to set up, to use, and also to restore from.

These programs are much easier to utilize than in the past and they are really inexpensive, so there's truly no good reason why you should not have every one of your data on your SQL server backed up all the time. With all the number of threats which are out there, giving your data to opportunity is a risky business, and you may discover one day that many of your information is gone.

Functions of SQL Database Backup Services Oftentimes, disaster is the case with our computers and our data gets quickly corrupted or lost. This might be due to viruses, human error, or calamities.

Nevertheless, whatever happens you must usually have a backup of your files. Thus, for anybody who's utilizing a laptop, a database backup is crucial. This might take time but in the long run, it will be for your best interest. SQL database backup solutions may be an alternative.

A number of functions of SQL repository backup.

1. It extracts and maintenance information from the SQL server that is been corrupted

2. It can recover main keys, indexes and.

3. It can develop a backup software file(s).

4. It restores and totally repairs big database.

5. It can recover deleted documents and save in a new SQL file.

6. It can recover procedures, tables, views, triggers.

7.upports recovery of SQL servers

Recovering data might be done on the internet or offline. Database restore may be hard and so the best thing to perform is to not wait for damage to occur. Make use of the countless SQL database backup offered live or you can back up the files manually.

How you can backup SQL database

• You have to initially have a chance to access asymmetric key certificate before you can begin restoring database so you must constantly keep the encryption element safe and protected.

• Connect to Microsoft SQL server motor, select pc user repository, choose and increase repository system.

• Click database, then simply click Task and Restore.

• Click the database which will in turn receptive the Restore Database dialog package. The specific restoring data source will appear in to Database show box, type the title in the show box.

• Utilizing the browse button press to a place in time text package, set a date and time and click Point on time restore box.

• Click From database, or From Device to pick the cause and place of database being restored. Click OK once you have included the equipment in the Backup location package, then choose the backup to bring power grid will show the backups offered you can alter the choice in grid.

• In the "select a site pane" click choice, then click select. Click restore option panel and select the choice which is ideal for your case.

• Also restore the database to an alternative place by choosing location in the Restore database grid. You can choose to - restore with healing, bring without any recovery, or restore with standby.

You can additionally watch video demonstrations that are online on how you can utilize SQL database backup. Nevertheless, you can begin utilizing an alternative backup, such as a USB or a disk to keep your data and files. You can utilize this in case you can't use SQL repository backup.

In case you have much more than a single personal computer you can additionally copy and transport your files on the different computers therefore in the event that your main computer is corrupted next you nonetheless have your data unchanged. SQL database backup is obviously the better choice for SQL servers.

CHAPTER 33

To Secure Your SQL Database With SQL Database Backup Technology

A large amount of individuals are searching for solutions to secure the SQL database. This is clear because this database contains important information. Without it, or if a thing goes wrong, an entire operation might stop to keep on.

To be able to stay away from this from happening for you or your company, you will need an sql database backup plan. Getting this particular system will allow you to quickly perform a database bring in any event that something fails with your system or in case your method is under attack. Without this, you are always in danger of losing your files and crucial data.

And so the question now is, how you can backup SQLdatabase to stay away from problems such as for instance excessive downtime in addition to permanent loss of information that is important.

The Answer to this issue is having a system which will allow you to immediately do sql database backup. These programs are plentiful on the web and the most elementary functions that they will provide you are the following:

- Program compatibility with many frequent operating systems today

- Capability to do SQL restore

- Support for nearly all of the present character sets

- Store and also save engines in addition to tables

- The capacity to backup crucial PHP and SQL files on various servers

These are probably the most popular and most simple functions which an SQL database backup application should have the ability to offer. Apart from that, the application should additionally have the ability to reply to the question of how you can backup SQL database by way of a well-constructed help menu.

It's typical for an automatic system which performs SQL database backup being a self-contained or self-reliant system. When you have installed the system and also you begin it up at first, you ought to be in a position to see an easy and simple to adopt setup wizard.

By means of this first stage, you can decide and alter the options of the system to tell it when you should do database restore, when to backup documents, what to backup, and a lot more. When you have completed this, everything should be accomplished automatically by the system.

A very good system will present you with an SQL server backup software you require not care about again after you have begun it. The moment something goes wrong, the concept is that the program will instantly kick in and restore that much files as it can to be able to minimize losses.

Even though you can perform your manual backups for every file in your SQL database that takes a lot of time and hand labor. This is a thing that quite a few people don't want. Of course, if nobody does it, odds are you will lose your data one of the ways or yet another.

With an application instantly do sql database backup, you'll don't have to stress about lost information and files once again. Simply be sure you select the proper program which will provide you with all of the functions that you need. It's equally vital that you be sure that the user interface is simple, understandable, and clear.

CHAPTER 34

SQL Reporting Services

SQL server reporting solutions is a component of the business intelligence stack, supplied by Microsoft. It enables you to produce extremely complicated accounts, a lot sooner (including charts, maps etc) and also to be seen in an internet browser.

Below is a feature summary of Microsoft SSRS, together with relatively information you have to be able to begin to learn Microsoft SSRS In the beginning you will need to set up, Adventure functions database. This is readily available at code plex. It has a great set of information that you can work with.

To be able to begin helping SSRS, you have to set up the necessary programs - i.e SQL server Database motor, Business Intelligence Development Studio (commonly termed as BIDS), Microsoft SSRS.

Let's check out a short overview SSRS and what will it offer for fast report development.

SSRS reports are plain xml documents, also known as report definition language or RDL .

SSRS enables reports to be exported with Microsoft Word, PDF CSV, Microsoft Excel, XML etc.

RDL's should additionally be seen using ASP.NET report viewer web settings. And also this means that, you produce reports with SSRS, and utilizing report viewer controls, you'll be able to embed in any ASP.NET site to render the SSRS reports.

For easier statement developments, SSRS supplies Report Builder. It is basically a software program which helps you to rapidly build SSRS report.

SSRS additionally enables you to program utilizing C# and VB, in case your needs aren't met in the built-in controls offered by SSRS.

SSRS enables you to develop complicated expressions, to represent your data in however type you need.

SSRS features a cool feature known as subscription. Which means that the moment you produce a report and deploy the same, you can provide the report either in an email format or lower it to any schedule and a fileshare.

SSRS also offers an excellent protection configuration. Most statement amount protection (who views the article and that doesn't) could be managed by an admin.

In case you have much more customers accessing your report, you can scale SSRS by deploying similar to a farm.

SSRS additionally exposes web services, also called as Report Server Web program. It's essentially an xml web program with a Soap API.

The newest version is Microsoft SQL server 2012 reporting. It's a lot of enhancements over the prior on - SQL server 2008 R2 Reporting.

You will find a few of equipment which ship together with SQL Server Reporting services 2012 including powerview, SQL azure reporting etc.

For Faster rendering of accounts, SSRS gives caching and snapshot option. You can plan Caching of reports or snapshotting a report and any interval. This can help in faster retrieval of reports.

SSRS additionally allows for sharepoint integration.

In addition to all of the characteristics mentioned above, it offers a really user favorable way to create/group/sort/add calculations/parameterize/administer information and in addition do adhoc reporting. It can likewise retrieve info from XML web service and also develop reports over it.

CHAPTER 35

Sql Replication With Online Backup

It's crucial that every company institute a disaster backup for its data stores. Your company's data contains much more than just e mail messages or simple Word documents ; it also consists of databases and site info.

Among the worst type of things which could occur to the business, whether it's small or large, is losing any of your electric data due to hardware disaster, software corruption, or to an all-natural disaster.

However all these three things happen much more than you might want to consider. Nevertheless, by being prepared you could be one step in front of the game.

In case you company utilizes an SQL database, it's very important you have frequent backups of the information. The very best exercise for just about any business is having a neighborhood message of the information and also offsite backup in case of any significant disaster to your physical building.

One of the greatest things you can do with the SQL data is replicating the information to a backup server and an offsite backup area. This would assure that your data is readily available should you actually have to restore it and there's some form of harm to your servers.

By creating a neighborhood copy you can do very simple restorations, and also by developing an offsite copy, you are discussed in case something occurs to your building.

Microsoft SQL Server allows you the capability to replicate the data to various other servers operating SQL Server, to be able to backup your database. This particular procedure lets you replicate your data to the next server at your company location, or through the web to some SQL server hosted by an internet information backup provider.

But if your local server must fail, you will have the capacity to revive it through one of your replicated copies and rapidly get your database back up and running.

Microsoft SQL Server provides 3 kinds of SQL replication. They are: merge replication, transactional replication and snapshot replication.

Snapshot replication just copies all database objects just as they are at any moment on time.

Transactional replication copies modifications into the database as they take place in real time.

Merge replication initially completes a picture replication after which follows it with transactional replication as information improvements.

SQL Server lets you effortlessly configure it to operate each of the 3 SQL replication methods with the web. This provides for you to have the ability to backup your data online just in case you actually have to bring it. The minimum acceptable backup will be a snapshot replication every night.

Among the most crucial things for your business success is its electronic data. The information your company generates every day has cost your organization both money and time. Trying to recreate information isn't everything you, as an entrepreneur, ever want to need to do.

So long as you prepare for the unforeseen and backup your data daily, you won't need to ever return and attempt to recreate your information from scratch. You can never be very prepared when disaster threatens your business.

CHAPTER 36

SQL Server Replication For Data Storage For Your Business

Database management systems are of all the most crucial software systems for organizations in the info age. SQL Server is an enterprise amount RDBMS supplied by Microsoft and it is popular in the business community.

SQL Server has the science which enables you to replicate your data to various servers therefore allowing your company information to be kept in much location - this procedure is called replication.

Replication is the procedure of sharing data involving databases in different locations. Implementing replication, you produce copies of the database and also discuss the copy with various users. This enables them making alterations to their local copy of the database and also later synchronize the changes to the cause website.

Database replication also can augment the disaster-recovery plans by copying the information from a neighborhood database server to a remote database server. Whenever the main server fails, your applications can switch to the replicated message of the information and continue operations.

You can instantly backup a database by having a replica on an alternative computer. Replication lets you continue making modifications online.

You can replicate a database on extra network servers and reassign subscribers to balance the lots across those servers.

Microsoft SQL server employs publishing market design to represent the pieces and tasks in replication architecture.

According to the publication version we can recognize the coming entities for the SQL Server replication version: Publisher, Publications, Subscriber, Articles, Agent, Distributor, and Subscriptions.

Publisher

Publisher is a server which makes the information for subscription to various other servers. And making data for replication, a publisher additionally identifies what data has transformed in the subscriber throughout the synchronizing process. Based on the kind of replication, changed information is identified at quite different instances. We will learn about Replication sorts in the Replication Types area.

Distributor

Distributor keeps the Distribution Database. The job of the distributor differs based on the kind of replication. Two kinds of Distributors are identified: Local distributor and remote distributor. Remote distributor is distinct from publisher and it is set up like a distributor for replication. Community distributor is a server which is configured as a distributor and a publisher.

Agents

Agents is the processes which are accountable for copying and distributing data between Subscriber and Publisher.

Subscriber

Subscriber is a server which receives and maintains the published information.

Articles

An article can be some database object, viz. Tables, Stored Procedures, Indexed views, Views, User defined operates.

Publication

Publication is a set of articles.

Subscriptions

Subscription can be a request for message of information or database items being replicated.

CHAPTER 37

Effective SQL Databases

Do not be tricked by seeming simplicity. A lot of developers get at ease with a particular method of developing a database for their web applications they miss out on methods they must prefer to employ making things run faster and better.

A lot of developers do not bear in mind which the little site they are creating right now may grow into something extremely big and complex, and the database they created is now bloated and does not scale nicely to meet up with the needs of the greater traffic.

This chapter hopes to offer web developers with a couple of methods to help make their database and queries faster and more effective.

1. Stay away from Character Types

When you are developing a database, it's very easy to establish all information kinds to the VARCHAR type because it can then include some information you want; text or numbers. But character information is amongst the most inefficient details type you can get. In case an area is just going to include numbers, then ensure it is among the correct kinds (INT, Double, etc).

Additionally, anywhere possible in your web development code, use numeric details sorts instead of characters. One of the more typical issues a script must keep are flags like if somebody answered yes or no to a question, etc. You might obviously stow it as' Y' or' N' but why don't you place it as zero and one?

The main reason this makes a difference happens when you have a database, for instance, with more than 500 zero entries, and therefore are operating a SELECT on that area, comparisons are processed a lot quicker for numeric details sorts than character types.

Furthermore, in case you have to go back information to the calling software, numeric details is less memory comprehensive than character information. Additionally, your web development language (PHP, ASP, etc) would likewise have the ability to approach and accomplish features on numeric details much better compared to character information.

I'm not trying to persuade you never ever to work with character data types. Occasionally it's a need, but in case you can discover ways to lessen the quantity of character information processed by your SQL database, the greater your server will cope.

2. Normalization

Normalizing a database is actually rather an intricate procedure. It's a method which describes a method to design a database framework to stay away from repetition of information in your database and will

result in substantial performance advantages when employed correctly. Nevertheless, the whole practice of normalisation is somewhat beyond the range of this particular chapter because it can fill up publications by itself, but any creator developing a database must really think about starting to be knowledgable about normalisation and also employing it in their own designs.

3. DateTime vs Timestamp fields

This really pertains to 1. a bit. The fundamental difference to take into account here's that an area of sort DATETIME is really stored as a number of characters. An area of sort TIMESTAMP is really saved as an integer. Hence, therefore, a more effective way of saving dates is utilizing the timestamp method. The timestamp has its drawbacks however.

For example, you can't store a date first compared to one January, 1970. Additionally, timestamps in your script will need recalculating to reach the character format. Due to this particular recalculation, it might not be advisable to store as timestamp. It actually is a case of examining which format works much better for your needs.

4. Use Limit anywhere possible

From your queries, in case you are performing a SELECT to some database and also you just expect a specific amount of outcomes, making use of the Limit declaration can speed your query up incredibly.

For instance, in case you have a table of consumers and also you have to operate a query to look for one people record, you can utilize a query like:

SELECT user_name from consumers Where user_id = 453; This query is absolutely legitimate and can get back the proper consequence. But additionally you know there'll just be One result.

The query above will search the database, find everything you need, however still continue searching after which. It will perform a lot quicker in case you might tell the query that after it's discovered what you are searching for to quit searching. Limit can accomplish this, as this particular query shows:

SELECT user_name from consumers Where user_id = 453 Limit one; Imagine this particular situation. You have a table named logins, which documents each login from a person.

It currently contains more than two zero zero records, and you need to discover the first time a person logged in. However remember that simply because this particular table inserts information over time, it's currently sorted for by date.

5. Stay away from utilizing LIKE

Assuming you have attempted to employ

1. above, and then ideally you will be in a scenario in which you don't have to use Like all very much. LIKE is among the most ineffective methods for searching a table. Just like functions a content comparison hunt in an area and without any wildcards is as effective as an immediate comparison; i.e. Where name =' Jane' is the same as Where title Like' Jane'. It's whenever you begin introducing the wildcard characters like' %' that things get truly hairy.

If you have make use of LIKE, then at least attempt to make effective use of the wildcards. These are' _' (underscore) and' %'. Allow me to explain all of this with a real life example.

In a task I was engaged in, we'd a SQL database keeping logs created instantly starting from a mail server. Regrettably, the mail server basically simply dumped a quite lengthy string of text data to an area that contained the information we wanted.

A software had being composed finding each logs which described a login by a person into the POP server. The sole manner we might do this was searching every history for a string at the msg area that had the content "User logged in" within it. The first query developed was something as this:

SELECT msg From logs Where msg Like' %User logged in %'; This query had taken on average of approximately thirty five mins to process. Clearly not the ideal situation.

The way in which the LIKE worked out here was it'd to parse through each and every portion of every single record in the msg area looking for text which matched "User logged in" anyplace in the text. We could figure out eventually the book "User logged in" occurred in the conclusion of that book at the msg area and so we changed the query:

SELECT msg From logs Where msg Like' %User logged in'; The' %' in the conclusion was eliminated as we don't desire to stress about copy after because there's not one. The query today just compares text to the string in the msg industry in the conclusion of the area and no longer parses with the whole portion of text kept in msg. The query nowadays ran in under two minutes.

Hopefully with each one of these components put into practice on a new web development project, you can have a database which operates fast, efficiently, uses as small sources as wont and possible grind to a stop whenever the load unexpectedly improves.

CONCLUSION

Many people cope with huge databases on a routine schedule. They are ordinarily companies that keep monitor of big portions of info and every one of it must be protected. If it was not protected, certain protocols or clientele data could be lost permanently.

Many of this material cannot be replaced quite easily, and it might put a company back a particular degree. This is exactly where an SQL backup application is available in handy, as it makes big database backups and will backup one file at once.

This will make certain all of your information is safe if the device fails. Most likely, you have some other types of backup fitted, but this can especially defend your database and most of the files. An SQL backup can help people who routinely deal with big databases. You will find choices in which you can do a file team backup and another enables you to deal with a single file.

This would call for a little preparation, but this is beneficial as a single file might be as large as some people's file team. It's additionally valuable since you will not wish to produce a complete backup all the time, due to all of the info. You will have to produce successive transaction log backups in case you wish to utilize a file team backup.

If you are using any of the final party programs, many of them enable you to record pictures of particular data.

This exclusively occurs with Storage Area Network solutions, since it enables you to replicate an entire data source from a single region to the next disk drive. Nevertheless, it is usually costly and it's to be planned in the outset of installation.

People who deal with big databases need to look into the SQL backup plan. It's one way of protecting your data.

www.ingramcontent.com/pod-product-compliance
Lightning Source LLC
Chambersburg PA
CBHW071131050326
40690CB00008B/1418